COULD THAT HAVE *BEEN* MORE HUMILIATING??

The Top Six Most Embarrassing Facts
About The Friends:

ROSS: He's referred to as "Bobo the Sperm Guy" by his ex-wife Carol and her lover, Susan.

MONICA: That's *her* underwear hanging from the telephone pole in front of her building (thanks to Fun Bobby).

RACHEL: At Mindy and Barry's wedding, she walks down the aisle with her dress caught in her pantyhose.

CHANDLER: While locked in an ATM vestibule during a blackout, he awkwardly tells supermodel Jill Goodacre, "Gum would be perfection."

JOEY: He lands the plum role of "butt double" for Al Pacino, but blows it by fighting with the director about his butt's motivation.

PHOEBE: She was once dumped by a guy because she fell asleep watching *This Is Spinal Tap.*

TRUE FRIENDS

The Official *TV Guide* Book

Unabridged, Unadulterated, and Completely Unauthorized

Amy Paulsen

HarperPaperbacks
A Division of HarperCollins*Publishers*

HarperPaperbacks
A Division of HarperCollins*Publishers*
10 East 53rd Street, New York, N.Y. 10022-5299

ISBN 0-06-101190-8

First printing: September 1996

Printed in the United States of America

❖ 10 9 8 7 6 5 4 3 2 1

This book is dedicated to my parents, Joe and Ann Paulsen, who always let me watch as much television as I wanted, perhaps secretly suspecting that it would pay off someday.

Special thanks go to *TV Guide* editor in chief Steven Reddicliffe, for giving me the opportunity to write this book, and to my *TV Guide* colleagues Stephanie Williams, Rick Schindler, and Vicki Clausman, without whose creative contributions this book would not exist.

I am also indebted to Sara Bethell and Rich Sands for all their helpful input, and to Lesly Atlas, my editor at HarperPaperbacks, who knows how to run a tight deadline.

As always, thank you to Bert, Nora, and Rosie for your patience, love, and support.

CONTENTS

Introduction

In the fall of 1995, the cast and creators of TV's hottest new sitcom approached their second season with fear and trepidation: "Yes, we've proven ourselves," a jittery Jennifer Aniston told *TV Guide*, "but I'm nervous about being able to keep it up."

"This year," added executive producer Kevin Bright, "it's about survival."

Someone should have told them to relax. *Friends* not only survived its second season, it once again slayed all of the sitcom competition, with the exception of its Thursday night neighbor, the unsinkable *Seinfeld.*

And keep it up they did. Season two was both satisfying—Ross and Rachel finally managed to connect—and full of surprises: Monica found love with an older man (Tom Selleck), Phoebe found a younger brother, Joey found fleeting fame, and Chandler found . . . Janice? And if you want to know more, well, that's why you bought this book. It's got sex. It's got drama. It's got star power. It's got Ugly

Naked People. So turn the page and get on with it already. Meanwhile, here are the

Top Six Predictions for Fall 1996

1. Rachel will get a new hairdo.
2. Ross will not.
3. Phoebe will find Pharmacist Frank (her dad).
4. Monica will make up, and then break up, with Dr. Richard Burke (Tom Selleck).
5. Joey will take acting lessons.
6. Chandler will dump Janice.

Amy Paulsen
Deputy editor, *TV Guide*

1

THE FRIENDS' FILES

ROSS EUSTACE GELLER (PLAYED BY DAVID SCHWIMMER)

After an entire first season of pining and pathos, this year Ross finally got what he wanted: Rachel (see "Ross and Rachel: Anatomy of a Romance," page 122). Of course, Ross's world doesn't revolve solely around Rachel, there's . . . let's see . . . ah, yes! There's his new son, Ben (who, like all good TV babies, is seldom seen or heard from). And there are dinosaur bones. And there's his new son, Ben. (Okay, we said that already.) And there's . . . well, actually there's not a whole lot else. But that doesn't matter, because Ross has Rachel. And right now that's all he needs.

ROSS AT WORK: A TIMELINE

Occupation:

Paleontologist at the American Museum of Natural History.

May 18, 1995:

The museum sends Ross to China for what he refers to as a "whole big bone thing."

Ross at Play: A Timeline

First Love:

Rachel, ever since ninth grade.

First Lover:

His ex-wife, Carol Willick, a sixth-grade teacher. Carol dumps Ross in the series pilot after explaining that she's a lesbian. (Phoebe's shrink boyfriend theorizes that Ross married her knowing she was a lesbian and that he may have wanted his marriage to fail because of "low self-esteem" or "to compensate for overshadowing a sibling.") In the episode following the pilot, Carol tells him she's pregnant.

Before We Met Him:

Ross liked a girl named Susan Salidor in college; when she asked him if Chandler was gay, Ross said yes, and that he was going out with Bernie Spellman (who also liked her). In 1989 he and Carol had sex behind a couple of mechanical Dutch children at Disneyland when the "It's a Small World After All" ride broke down.

October 20, 1994:

Ross goes to a coin laundry with Rachel, which Chandler insists qualifies as a date.

January 5, 1995:

Ross plays "tonsil tennis" with Chandler's mom (Morgan Fairchild) at a Mexican restaurant after several rounds of tequila shots.

February 9, 1995:

Urged on by the guys, Ross asks out a woman named Kristen Riggs who lives in his building and once borrowed an egg from him. It's his first date in nine years, so he takes her to a Japanese hibachi restaurant where he and Carol used to go. And, gee, what a surprise! Who should turn up at the same table but Carol and her lover?

February 16, 1995:

Ross goes out with Celia, a coworker at the museum. The relationship seems promising, but they can't seem to get past the cuddling stage. On their first date, Ross introduces Celia to his monkey, Marcel, and the two don't get along. Then Celia asks Ross to talk dirty to her, and he chokes. On the next date, Ross talks dirty to her for hours (he's been prepped by Joey), but by the time he's done they're too exhausted to do anything but cuddle.

March 3, 1995:

Chandler asks why Ross hasn't gone out again with a woman named Linda. Ross explains that it's not just because of her "whole *The Flintstones*-could've-really-happened thing." The reason, of course, is Rachel.

May 18, 1995:

Ross returns from China and, like most travelers, he's brought back some cool new stuff—including a girlfriend named Julie. The two knew each other in grad school (she's a paleontologist, too) and they ran into each other at the "big bone thing" in China.

October 12, 1995:

Ross finally gets to have sex with a woman who's not Carol. (It's Julie.)

November 9, 1995:

Ross finds out that Rachel is indeed interested in him. The two exchange their first major blowout kiss—despite the fact that Ross is still going out with Julie.

November 16, 1995:

Ross dumps Julie for Rachel. Rachel is thrilled—until she sees "the List."

February 1, 1996:

Rachel forgives Ross. It's official: they're a couple.

February 8, 1996:

Rachel and Ross are not only a couple, they are now an *intimate* couple.

May 16, 1996:

Ross kisses Joey, trying to help him practice for a part that requires him to kiss another man. After the kiss, he finds out that Joey has already auditioned and lost the part.

Family

Ross is the pride and joy of his parents, Jack and Judy Geller. His sister, Monica, is not.

Special Talent

Tenacity.

Six Embarrassing Facts About Ross

1. Ross is referred to as "Bobo the Sperm Guy" by his ex-wife, Carol, and her lover, Susan.
2. He believed his parents when they told him that his dog, Chi Chi, had been sent to the Milners' farm in Connecticut.
3. He mistakes his ex-wife's friend Tanya for Huey Lewis.

4. He can't see the Magic Eye stereograms.
5. He's allergic to lobster, peanuts, and kiwi fruit.
6. He's afraid of needles.

	DAVID SCHWIMMER	ROSS GELLER
Early Years:	Chubby high-school nerd	High-school nerd with chubby sister
Career Crossroads:	Enrolled in high school drama class on a whim	Majored in paleontology on a dare
Education:	B.S. in speech and theater	Ph.D. in paleontology
Former Roommate:	Joey Slotnick (who plays Sam on The Single Guy)	Marcel (monkey)
Girlfriend:	Attorney from Louisiana (former)	Waitress at Central Perk (current)

MONICA LILLIAN GELLER
(PLAYED BY COURTENEY COX)

For a pathological perfectionist, Monica leads a remarkably flawed existence. In fact, if she had to take stock of her life right now, she'd be a high-risk candidate for a nervous breakdown. Over the course of one year, she has lost both the perfect job *and* the perfect man. But Monica has also proven herself to be a trouper this year, and if she did have a nervous breakdown, it would probably be a very tidy, short-lived affair. Just look how well she's handling her current job crisis: After a brief, unsuccessful attempt at mastering the stock market, she swallowed her pride and took a job as a waitress at a fifties theme restaurant. Yes, it's demeaning that she has to dance whenever anyone puts a quarter in the jukebox, but the perverse pleasure she gives her friends as they watch her shimmy in her poodle skirt is nothing short of . . . perfection.

MONICA AT WORK: A TIMELINE

Occupation:
Chef.

Before We Met Her:

Monica was a sous chef at Manhattan's Café des Artistes. When the series begins, she is assistant chef at the trendy Upper West Side restaurant Iridium.

February 16, 1995:

One of Phoebe's massage clients is opening a restaurant, so Phoebe arranges a chef audition for Monica. Monica cooks up a storm, but it's all for naught when the restaurant guy (Jon Lovitz) shows up stoned and in the mood for a junk-food munchfest. (Between bites of taco shells, he does manage to sample one of Monica's dishes, and he likes it well enough to shout, "Slap my ass and call me Judy!")

April 17, 1995:

Monica and Fake Monica (the woman who stole her credit cards) audition for *Cats*. Monica gets to sing only two notes ("Mem-o—").

October 19, 1995:

Monica gets promoted to head lunch chef and head of purchasing, then gets fired when she accepts five steaks from her new meat supplier. "That was *not* a kickback," she tells her boss over the phone. "Okay, what, what is a kickback? . . . Okay, so it's a kickback."

November 9, 1995:

Monica volunteers to be Chandler's personal fitness trainer.

November 16, 1995:

Monica gets a job, kind of: creating holiday recipes for a chalky, crumbly synthetic chocolate called Mockolate (which, she accidentally discovers, can clean aluminum).

January 18, 1995:

Monica is thrilled when Carol and Susan's wedding caterer has a bike wreck—that means *she* gets the job!

February 1, 1996:

At a chef audition Monica attempts to make a salad but calls it quits when the restaurant manager turns out to be a food pervert (he tells her he likes the lettuce dirty and wonders whether the tomatoes are bad—"very, *very* bad?").

February 8, 1996:

Monica caters a party for her parents' friend Dr. Richard Burke (see "Monica at Play," below).

April 25, 1996:

Monica invests the last of her life savings in the stock market. She buys shares of such stocks as CHP (because she used to have a crush on Erik Estrada) and ZXY (because it sounds "zexy"). She loses her money and is reduced to taking a job at a theme diner, where she has to dress up, dance, and wear "flame-retardant boobs!"

Amy Paulsen

MONICA AT PLAY: A TIMELINE

Before We Met Her:

Monica got *around*. She had a schoolgirl crush on Tommy Rollerson (Rachel once put a valentine with his name on it in her locker). She had a high-school sweetheart named Teddy who dumped her because she was fat. Her prom date, Roy Gublick, touched one of her boobs when he pinned on her corsage. She claims she "did it" on a pool table during her senior year of college. She had a crush on Joey when he first moved in with Chandler, and she was once set up with Joey's cousin, "who could belch the alphabet." Her other boyfriends include Jason Hurley, whom Phoebe slept with right after Monica broke up with him; Kevin Milmore, whom she actually *enjoyed* breaking up with ("May he rot in hell"); and Steve, who lisped.

September 22, 1994:

Monica has a date with Paul the Wine Guy, who tells her he hasn't been able to perform since his wife left him. Like a fool, she believes him—and tries to help.

October 6, 1994:

Monica is seeing a guy named Alan, whose charms include his crooked smile, his "pimiento trick" with olives, and his mean David Hasselhoff impression. All the Friends love him (especially when he helps them win a softball game against the Hasidic jewelers)—except Monica.

October 20, 1994:

Monica helps Joey reunite with his ex-girlfriend Angela by hitting on Angela's current boyfriend, Bob.

December 15, 1994:

Monica asks her old boyfriend Fun Bobby to be her New Year's Eve date. "He's like a party with legs," Chandler says. But when Fun Bobby arrives at the party, he announces that his grandfather just died, and spends the rest of the evening in Bereaved Bobby mode.

January 5, 1995:

Monica whistles at a hot guy—he turns to flirt with her and is hit by an ambulance. While he lies in a coma, she decides he's her dream man: "a lawyer who teaches sculpting on the side. And he can *dance.*" The romance ends when Coma Guy awakens and falls short of expectations.

February 9, 1995:

Phoebe mentions Monica's ex-boyfriend Howard the Winner, who used to scream "I win!" during sex. And Monica reminisces about her old boyfriend Trekkie Guy, who told her while they were making out that he wanted "to boldly go where no man has gone before." To uncelebrate Valentine's Day, the girls build a boyfriend bonfire, and Monica burns a nude picture of one Scotty Jarad. The firemen soon arrive to put out the flames, and before they're done, dates have been made all around. The girls decide that maybe men aren't so horrible after all—but what they don't know yet is that their prospective dates are all married.

February 23, 1995:

Rachel and Monica go out with the two sexy doctors who treated Rachel's twisted ankle (*ER*'s George Clooney and Noah Wyle). But since the girls have assumed each other's identities (Rachel pretended to be Monica at the hospital so she could use her health insurance), the evening gets a little weird. (Rachel as Monica: "I use my breasts to get people's attention." Monica as Rachel: "Hey, we both do that!")

April 27, 1995:

Monica and Fake Monica crash some kind of "embassy party" and Monica kisses someone she thinks was an archbishop, although "it could have been a chef."

May 4, 1995:

Monica dates (and deflowers) Young Ethan, a seventeen-year-old high-school senior who lies about his age. (So does Monica, who finally confesses that she's "twenty-five—and thirteen months.") She totally freaks out when she realizes she "had sex with someone who wasn't alive during the Bicentennial!"

October 19, 1995:

Monica gets a hickey from a Blowfish after a Hootie & the Blowfish concert.

January 4, 1996:

Monica reunites with Fun Bobby and gets him to stop drinking. Overnight, Fun Bobby turns into Boring Bobby, and Monica is driven to drink just to put up with his tedious droning. By the end of the episode, Bobby breaks up with Monica because he feels *she* has a drinking problem.

January 28, 1996:

Monica and Rachel create a love triangle with Jean-Claude Van Damme: Monica likes him, he likes Rachel. By the episode's end, the Muscles from Brussels decides he likes both and suggests a threesome. Grossed out but flattered, the girls politely decline.

February 8, 1996:

Monica falls for her parents' good friend Dr. Richard Burke (Tom Selleck). They're the perfect couple, except for that darned age difference (Monica: "I'm dating a man whose pool I once peed in").

May 16, 1996:

Monica and Richard discuss kids: she wants 'em, he doesn't. (He's been there, done that. In fact, he's a grandfather.) And though he says he'd be willing to start the whole family thing all over again just to be with her, she sadly declines the offer. Bye-bye, love.

Family

Monica's brother, Ross, is the pride and joy of their parents, Jack and Judy Geller. Monica is not.

Special Talents

Monica can take off her bra with her clothes on. And she can whip Chandler and Joey at Foosball.

Seven Embarrassing Facts about Monica

1. She's called "our little harmonica" by her parents.
2. She was a fat kid who spent a lot of time in her room reading and doing puzzles.
3. That's *her* underwear hanging from the telephone pole in front of her apartment building (thanks to Fun Bobby).
4. She was trapped in the bathroom while her parents made out at her dad's birthday party.

5. She played a nun in a high-school performance of *The Sound of Music.*
6. She spent $69.95 for a Wonder Mop.
7. She used to have a cat named Fluffy Meowington.

Twelve Rules to Live By (If You Want to Be Just Like Monica)

1. Don't allow monkeys to play with spatulas.
2. Pay bills on time.
3. Buy only laundry detergent that comes in containers with easy-to-pour spouts.
4. Coasters are there for a reason.
5. Teflon pans must be cleaned only with a plastic scrubber.
6. Take down the notes on the fridge when they're out of date.
7. When replacing a cap on a Magic Marker, make sure to push the cap until you hear the click.
8. Toilet paper should be folded into a point.
9. Pennies must be rolled "as soon as there are a hundred in the dish."
10. Always fold the end of the duct tape into a little tab.
11. Keep items on a desk perpendicular to one another: "If it's not a right angle, it's a wrong angle."
12. Set the bedroom clock six minutes fast.

Amy Paulsen

A *TV Guide* Q&A with Courtney Cox and Tom Selleck

TV Guide: You two have great chemistry. Explain it.

Courteney Cox: I truthfully think that Tom is the easiest person to work with. The most laid-back, easygoing—

Tom Selleck: But really churning and dynamic inside.

C.C.: Dynamic, I think, on the outside as well. The churning part I don't see.

TV Guide: Tom, did you feel a little bit like the outsider when you came in?

T.S.: It's scary, coming on a show. It's not a hostile environment, but I was the new guy.

C.C.: We are such a . . . I don't want to say clique, but we are a very tightly knit group. So that's got to be a hard situation.

TV Guide: The first time you came on the show, did the audience know you were going to be on?

T.S.: No. They kept me backstage. I had to walk through this kitchen door, and at that point I wanted to be on Pluto. I didn't want to go through that door.

C.C.: We were trying to be protective. Because [the set we were on] was not in front of the audience, it was off to the side. So I said to him, "Listen, maybe they will go nuts if they see you. But they may *not* see you. So don't be disappointed if they don't." He didn't even get a foot in the door and the audience saw him and they just went nuts.

TV Guide: Have either of you been in a romantic relationship like Monica and Richard's, where there is a real age difference?

C.C.: I have never *not* had one. I have only dated older men. I'm attracted to older men because of the knowledge and the experiences they have had. And I am a pretty domineering person, so I like a man older than me who can kind of put me back in my place . . . I like someone who has very strong opinions. Because if I can mold you, you are not interesting to me.

T.S.: You know, we don't grow up when we're twenty-one. I just don't think men are ready for a lot of things when they're young, and I'm not just talking about commitment. Women look at life differently early on, and it takes time for the two sexes to catch up.

TV Guide: Tom, do you feel like a new generation of people is discovering you because of *Friends?*

T.S.: Well, I *am* very cool with my adolescent nephews and nieces now.

	COURTENEY COX	MONICA GELLER
Musical Credentials:	Danced in Bruce Springsteen's video "Dancing in the Dark"	Dances at theme restaurant
Painful Adolescence:	Former teenage Misfit of Science	Formerly chubby teenage misfit
Men in Her Life:	Michael J. Fox (as Alex Keaton), Michael Keaton (as himself)	Tom Selleck (as Richard) Jean-Claude Van Damme (as himself)
Obsession:	Neat freak	Neat freak
Past Employment:	*Family Ties*, *Ace Ventura: Pet Detective*	Café des Artistes, Iridium

RACHEL KAREN GREEN (PLAYED BY JENNIFER ANISTON)

If there's one thing we've learned from season two of *Friends,* it's this: Rachel is more than just a great hairdo. Her romance with Ross shows that she's capable of great passion. Her distress over her parents' impending divorce shows that she's capable of great sorrow. And her appearance at her ex-fiancé's wedding shows that she's capable of great courage.

But seeing Rachel in this new light leads to a disturbing question: Why is she still working at Central Perk? Her ineptitude there shows that she is definitely not capable of great waitressing. Surely that fact must be sinking in by now, and if so, what is she waiting for? Rachel, you've got your love. Now go out there and get a *life.*

RACHEL AT WORK: A TIMELINE

Occupation:

None. Rachel is currently a waitress at Central Perk. She describes her job as foaming milk, wiping tables, writing specials on the board, and "sometimes Arturo lets me put the chocolate blobbies on the cookies."

October 20, 1994:

Rachel, who's never worked a day in her life, gets her first paycheck from Central Perk. "Look at the little window. There's my name," she says. "Hi, me!" But she gets a little upset when she sees how little the numbers are.

November 17, 1994:

Rachel asks her boss, Terry, for a $100 advance. He tells her, "You are a terrible, terrible waitress. Really awful." After he implies that she may not be working there long enough to justify an advance, she promises to try harder.

February 9, 1995:

Monica pays Rachel $20 an hour to waitress for her during a cooking audition after the "real waitress" she's hired bails at the last minute.

March 2, 1995:

After six months of work, Rachel is sick of being called "Excuse Me," so she sends out dozens of résumés (including one to *Popular Mechanics*). Even though the résumés contain typos—they mention her "excellent compuper skills"—she still manages to get an interview for a job as an assistant buyer at Saks Fifth Avenue. "It's like the mother ship is calling you home," Phoebe says. Rachel aces the interview—but the job still goes to somebody else.

RACHEL AT PLAY: A TIMELINE

Before We Met Her:

Rachel was engaged to an orthodontist, Dr. Barry Farber, but she left him at the altar because she realized it was his money she was after, and because he bore a likeness to Mr. Potato Head. Pre-Barry, she slept with a guy named Billy Dreskin on her parents' bed.

September 22, 1994:

In the very first episode, Rachel gets hit on twice: once by Joey and once by Ross.

November 3, 1994:

Rachel and Ross find a runaway cat during a blackout, which leads Rachel into the arms of the cat's owner: Paolo, her sexy Italian neighbor. By their sixth date, Paolo has already named her breasts.

January 12, 1995:

At this point Rachel and Paolo "are way past fling," and they plan a trip to the Poconos. But the trip gets canceled when Paolo makes a pass at Phoebe. Rachel breaks up with him and begins her famous "penis embargo."

February 9, 1995:

At the girls' boyfriend bonfire, Rachel immolates letters from Barry, boxers from Adam Ritter, and grappa from Paolo.

February 23, 1995:

Rachel and Monica set up a double date with a pair of gorgeous doctors (*ER*'s George Clooney and Noah Wyle). Thanks to the girls' odd behavior, romantic sparks fail to fly.

March 9, 1995:

Rachel's ex-fiancé, Barry, comes back into her life and tells her he still wants her—even though he's now engaged to her ex–maid of honor, Mindy.

April 6, 1995:

Rachel starts sleeping with Barry again; after a tryst in his office she exclaims, "It's so nice having the little sink here." But then she discovers that he cheated on her with Mindy while they were engaged, and she concludes that he's "Satan in a smock."

May 11, 1995:

Rachel flirts with Ross's ex-wife's obstetrician, Dr. Franzblau (Jonathan Silverman), in the delivery room. But the romance ends even before the baby is born, when Dr. Franzblau mentions how tired he sometimes gets of female anatomy.

May 18, 1995:

It's Rachel's birthday, and she goes out for a drink with Carl, a guy she met at the coffeehouse. Later, at her party, she finally learns the truth about

Ross. Since Ross is off to China, she keeps another date with Carl—and fantasizes about Ross the entire time.

September 21, 1995:

Rachel, devastated by the fact that Ross has a new girlfriend, sleeps with Paolo on the rebound. She says she "just happened to bump into him last night . . . in his apartment."

November 9, 1995:

Monica fixes Rachel up with Michael, a divorced guy; Rachel gets drunk during their dinner date and calls Ross. By the end of the episode, she and Ross are a love thing.

November 16, 1995:

It looks like all systems are go for Ross and Rachel—until she discovers his list comparing her to Julie.

January 4, 1996:

Rachel dates Russ, a virtual twin to Ross (the only difference: Russ is a periodontist, whereas Ross is a paleontologist). She ends it when she sees the resemblance.

January 28, 1996:

Rachel, trying to set Monica up with Jean-Claude Van Damme, accidentally sets *herself* up. They go to a place called Crossroads and hang out with Drew Barrymore.

February 1, 1996:

Rachel and Ross are reunited (and it feels so good).

February 8, 1996:

Rachel and Ross get naked at the American Museum of Natural History.

March 21, 1996:

While listing the guys she's slept with, Rachel counts Pete Carney—a guy who was referred to as *Phoebe's* ex-boyfriend (Pete the Weeper) in an earlier episode.

March 28, 1996:

Monica accuses Rachel of betraying her with Danny Arshack at a make-out party back in ninth grade, saying, "The bottle was totally pointing at *me*!"

FAMILY

Rachel has at least two sisters. One is named Jill, and one is about to graduate from college. Her father is a vascular surgeon and her mother is a Rachel wanna-be.

Special Talents

Rachel was class president, homecoming queen, *and* prom queen at Lincoln High School.

Six Embarrassing Facts About Rachel

1. When she hears the name George Stephanopoulos, she says, "Who's George Snuffelupagus?"
2. She peed in her pants in the seventh grade because Monica made her laugh.
3. She sang "Copacabana" in front of the whole school during the eighth-grade talent show but freaked out right in the middle.
4. She walked around with floss in her hair after doing it with Barry in his dentist's chair.
5. There's a nasty rumor going around that Rachel didn't marry Barry because she was suffering from syphillis.
6. At Mindy and Barry's wedding, she walks down the aisle with her dress caught in her pantyhose.

Rachel: Portrait of a Wretched Waitress

October 6, 1994:

Rachel distributes a decaf cappuccino, a black coffee, a lattè, and an iced tea among the Friends, then pats herself on the back for "getting pretty good at this." The minute she leaves, everybody exchanges drinks.

October 20, 1994:

Rachel's bad mood scares Ross out of ordering the dessert he wants. ("Or else I'll just have a big bowl of dirt," he says.)

November 17, 1994:

Rachel asks, "Anybody need coffee?" and everybody in the coffeehouse raises their hand. She asks a patron for an advance on her tips—and then apologizes for "the spill." She also breaks a cup.

December 15, 1994:

She serves Joey a cup of coffee that's so full he can't put milk in it. When he complains, she slurps some off the top and says, "Now there's room."

January 12, 1995:

When a customer asks for a round of cappuccinos, it takes Rachel a moment to realize he's talking to *her.*

January 19, 1995:

Rachel refuses to serve Chandler because she's mad at him for walking into her apartment and seeing her "boobies."

February 16, 1995:

Rachel serves Monica a hot cider with an pencil in it (the cinnamon stick is behind her ear).

March 9, 1995:

Rachel proudly recites the long list of tea varieties that the coffeehouse serves—to a guy who doesn't want tea.

September 21, 1995:

Rachel again refuses to serve Chandler. This time she's mad at him for the whole Ross fiasco. She also serves Ross a lemonade instead of the coffee he ordered.

January 4, 1996:

Rachel serves Monica cappuccino with regular milk instead of nonfat and won't take it back.

January 18, 1996:

Rachel brings a tray of used beverages over to her friends and says, "Who ordered what?" Ross says he ordered the "half-drunk cappuccino with the lipstick on the rim," and Chandler asks, "The thing with the cigarette butt in it . . . is that decaf?"

February 22, 1996:

Rachel drops a piece of pie into the hood of a patron's coat; a gallant Ross rescues it.

	JENNIFER ANISTON	RACHEL GREEN
Moneyed Background:	Father is a soap actor who plays a wealthy publisher	Father is a wealthy surgeon
Family Heartbreak:	Parents divorced when she was nine	Parents currently divorcing
Computer Background:	Appeared in Windows 95 tutorial; has her own Internet newsgroup and Web site	Résumé cites her "excellent compuper skills"; has her personal qualities listed on Chandler's computer
Ethnic Background:	Greek from the Valley	Jewish from Long Island
Enjoys:	Hiking and camping	Shopping at Saks

CHANDLER BING (PLAYED BY MATTHEW PERRY)

Could this season have *been* any more humiliating for Chandler? He gets teased by his friends about his third nipple, and he gets taunted by mean bullies at Central Perk. He gets scorned by a woman he just seduced, and he gets saddled with Eddie, the roommate from hell. He gets stuck wearing a really ugly bracelet, and he gets stranded in a men's room . . . wearing nothing but a pair of hot pink panties.

For someone who's such a smartass, Chandler spends way too much time playing the fool. To his credit, he realizes this, and he knows he's got to make some changes in his life if he doesn't want to end up like that other former smartass, Mr. Heckles: crazy, alone, and dead. Desperate, he tries to get back together with his old girlfriend, the painfully obnoxious Janice. Their reunion is less than successful: Janice is married and pregnant. At last season's end, Chandler makes one more attempt to find meaning in his life and searches cyberspace for his soul mate. He actually finds her there and arranges to meet her at Central Perk. As he waits for her with his friends, the tension mounts: Will she be old? Will she be ugly or will she be the woman of his dreams? But when she arrives, she's none of these things. She's Janice. Like we said, could this season have *been* any more humiliating for Chandler?

Chandler at Work: A Timeline

Occupation:

When the series starts, Chandler is a permanent temp at a data processing firm. He has been there for five years.

October 6, 1994:

Chandler makes a quick seven thousand bucks from Phoebe when he agrees to quit smoking. (She received the money from a soda company when she found a thumb in a can.)

February 16, 1995:

Big Al Kostelic promotes Chandler to processing supervisor, but Chandler quits rather than accept that his life's work is "worrying about the WENUS [Weekly Estimated Net Use of the System]." He goes to a career counselor, who tells him he's destined to be . . . a data processor. Chandler goes back to the office and takes the promotion.

February 23, 1995:

Chandler is given his first management task: fire Nina Bookbinder, who's been screwing not only with his WENUS but with the company's ANUS (Annual Net Usage Statistics). There's just one problem—she's too darned cute. Instead of canning her, he asks her out and then covers for himself at the office by saying Nina has psychological problems and can't remember being fired. When Nina confronts him, he proposes and then finally tells her the truth.

May 4, 1995:

When Phoebe temps as Chandler's secretary, she discovers that none of his work buddies like him anymore now that he's the boss. He goes out with them after work to show that he's still "one of them," but it only makes matters worse. He's the boss. He's "Mr. Bing– Boss Man Bing."

CHANDLER AT PLAY: A TIMELINE

October 20, 1994:

Chandler dumps his on-again, off-again girlfriend Janice just after she gives him a pair of Bullwinkle socks. It's part of a breakup pact with Phoebe, who dumps a guy named Tony. Janice tells him his real problem is his fear of commitment. She's right.

October 27, 1994:

Chandler goes to the theater to see Joey in *Freud!* and meets the lovely Aurora, a former member of the

Israeli army. He might be willing to make a commitment with her, but she's already committed to several others: her husband and a handful of boyfriends. Chandler can't hack it.

November 3, 1994:

Lucky dog Chandler gets stuck in an ATM vestibule with supermodel Jill Goodacre during a blackout. But he chokes, both literally (on a piece of gum) and figuratively (while trying to flirt with her). Still, she kisses him good-night.

November 10, 1994:

A coworker tries to set Chandler up—with another guy. None of his friends are surprised at his being mistaken for gay; as Phoebe points out, he has "homosexual hair."

December 15, 1994:

Chandler is so lonely that he invites Janice to spend New Year's Eve with him. But she drives him crazy and he dumps her again before midnight. Chandler does, however, get a New Year's kiss—from Joey.

January 19, 1995:

It is revealed that Chandler once had a girlfriend named Judy who ate Phoebe's makeup.

February 9, 1995:

Chandler goes along on a double date with Joey only to discover he's been set up with . . . Janice. They get drunk and end up in bed together. In the morning, a hung-over Chandler can't believe his bad luck.

February 23, 1995:

The Nina Bookbinder fiasco occurs (see "Work," above), netting Chandler one failed wedding proposal and a staple in his hand. (Hell hath no fury like a woman fired.)

April 6, 1995:

Chandler goes on a first date so fantastic that "years from now, schoolchildren will study it as one of the great first dates of all time." He calls Danielle the very next day and is tortured when she doesn't call him back. Is it him or is it his phone? Or *her* phone? Finally she tracks him down at Central Perk—an act he finds "too needy." It's all over.

October 5, 1995:

Chandler's friends criticize him for finding fault with every woman he dates. There was Joan, dumped because her nostrils were too big ("She leaned back and I saw her brain"). There was Maureen Rosillo, dumped because she didn't hate Yanni. There was Janice, dumped over and over because she was obnoxious. Still, Chandler decides to call Janice ("my last chance to have somebody"). But, as mentioned earlier, she is both married and pregnant. Next Chandler makes a date with his workmate Alison, someone he's avoided in the past because he found her head a little large. On the date, he realizes her head is in fact *huge*: "It's like I'm on a date with a Peanuts character."

October 19, 1995:

Chandler meets and sleeps with Jade, who accidentally called his number looking for Bob. When she calls again looking for Bob, she reveals that she found Chandler lacking in the bedroom. "It was just so awkward and . . . bumpy."

November 2, 1995:

While babysitting for little Ben, Chandler and Joey try to hit on Caroline (Lea Thompson), but she assumes that he and Joey are gay parents. Later, the boys try to hit on two women they meet on a bus and end up leaving baby Ben behind.

January 28, 1996:

Chandler runs into gorgeous Susie Moss (Julia Roberts) on the set of Marcel the monkey's new movie. It turns out they were in fourth grade together. And since he pulled up her skirt during the school play, she decides to get revenge, big time. After conning him into wearing her panties, she lures him into a men's room and tells him to strip. Excited, he obeys. She grabs his clothes and splits. (Correction: Hell hath no fury like a woman humiliated in the fourth grade.)

February 1, 1996:

Chandler introduces himself to a cute girl at the coffeehouse. She finds him charming and funny—until she spots that nasty gold bracelet hanging on his wrist.

March 21, 1996:

Chandler tells his new roommate, Eddie, that he once broke up with a woman who "actually thought Sean Penn was the capital of Cambodia." (Chandler also admits to not actually knowing what the capital of Cambodia is.)

May 2, 1996:

At Rachel's birthday party, a gorgeous woman mistakes him for a guy named Dennis and sticks her tongue down his throat. He doesn't correct her misapprehension.

May 16, 1996:

Chandler falls in love with his sexy new cyberpal. So he sets up a meeting with her and is shocked when he discovers that she's Janice! Oh, noooooo!

Family

Chandler is an only child whose parents divorced when he was nine; they announced the split at Thanksgiving dinner, right after he finished his pumpkin pie. His father drank heavily, and his mother is a romance novelist.

Special Talents

Chandler can imitate Mr. Rogers, Mr. Rourke, *and* Mr. T.

Ten Embarrassing Facts about Chandler

1. The third-nipple business.
2. He was once bitten by a peacock at the zoo.
3. He tells Jill Goodacre, "Gum would be perfection."
4. He has worn ladies' panties.
5. On *The Tonight Show*, his mom tells the world she bought him his first condoms.
6. His mom tells his friends that he wore her pearls when he was three.
7. He once left a message on someone's answering machine that included the phrase "Yes, indeedy-o."
8. He ties a towel around his head after he showers. "It's a leave-in conditioner, okay?"

9. He wore a denim cap with little mirrors on it in the fourth grade.
10. At boarding school, he had a growth spurt that affected only his arms. This resulted in his being called "Arm Guy" and "Mr. Big Arms."

Note to Chandler: Questions to Ask Prospective Roommates Before You Let Them Move In

1. Do you own a food dehydrator?
2. True or false: It's perfectly normal to watch your roommate as he sleeps.
3. Have you ever in your life mistaken a Pepperidge Farm goldfish for a living goldfish?
4. Are you tempted to steal mannequin heads from Macy's?
5. Are you a psycho?
6. Is your name Eddie?

   Bonus question: How do you feel about Foosball and *Baywatch*?

	Matthew Perry	Chandler Bing
Family:	Parents divorced when he was less than a year old	Parents divorced when he was nine

	MATTHEW PERRY	CHANDLER BING
Formative experience:	Got hooked on acting in seventh-grade school play	Pulled up classmate's skirt in fourth-grade school play
Favorite Sports:	Playing tennis, ice hockey	Playing Foosball; watching ice hockey, midget wrestling
Taste in Decorating:	Giant TV in living room; Foosball table in dining room	Giant TV in living room; Foosball table in dining room
Love Life:	Had brief fling with Julia Roberts	Had fling in Julia Roberts's briefs

JOEY MARCELLO TRIBBIANI, JR. (PLAYED BY MATT LEBLANC)

It's been said that Joey is no brain surgeon—but at least this year he got to play one on TV. In January Joey finally landed the part of a lifetime: Dr. Drake Ramoray, neurosurgeon extraordinaire, on the NBC soap opera *Days of Our Lives.* Joey is so successful in the role that he gets "his very own stalker," the beautiful but deranged Erika Ford, who believes Joey actually *is* Dr. Ramoray. And since Erika is so hot (to borrow a popular Joey adjective), he indulges her fantasy. Of course, pretending you're a brain surgeon when you're just a Joey can get tricky. While on a dinner date with Erika, he has some explaining to do after he refuses to assist a choking victim. (He does so with dazzling doctor-speak: "I'm a neurosurgeon, and that was a case of, uh, foodal chokage.")

Joey's soap stud status also leads to his sudden departure from the Bing-Tribbiani bachelor pad into a fabulous uptown apartment, where he can spend some quality time alone with his thoughts. But just when he's all settled in, bad news comes knocking: Dr. Ramoray is scripted to meet a tragic and untimely end. Out of work and out of money, Joey moves back in with Chandler, saddened by this setback but happy to be reunited with his bud. And as far as losing that quality time with his thoughts goes, Joey has no regrets: "Turns out I don't have as many thoughts as you'd think."

JOEY AT WORK: A TIMELINE

Occupation:

Actor/model.

Before We Met Him:

Joey appeared in a Wee Ones production of *Pinocchio,* was the Aramis Guy at Macy's, and made a commercial for Super Pizza in Queens, which aired during a broadcast of *Gandhi.* (His grandmother thought it was part of the movie and told the whole neighborhood, "Joey's in *Gandhi*!")

October 6, 1994:

Joey has to learn how to smoke to prepare for an audition. Chandler coaches him: "Now let your wrist go. Uh, not so much. Now try taking a puff."

October 27, 1994:

Joey appears in the lead role of the musical *Freud!* His performance lands him an agent named Estelle Leonard. His next job is as a "butt double" for Al Pacino, but he blows it by fighting with the director about his butt's motivation. "I got fired," he tells his friends. "They said I overacted with it."

November 17, 1994:

Joey models for a public-service announcement. To his dismay, he turns out to be the poster boy for venereal disease. His handsome face is accompanied by the slogan "You Never Know Who Might Have VD."

December 15, 1994:

After losing out on the part of a department store Santa, Joey accepts a lesser role as one of Santa's helpers.

April 27, 1995:

At Chandler's urging, Joey tries a new stage name: Joe Stalin. At the end of the episode, he switches to Holden McGroin and reads for the role of Mercutio in *Romeo and Juliet.*

May 18, 1995:

Joey volunteers to participate in a fertility study at NYU's medical school. It means seven hundred bucks for two weeks' work ("You're gonna be making money hand over fist," exclaims Phoebe), but it does put a crimp in his love life.

September 28, 1995:

Joey takes on a department store day job as the Bijan for Men Man. Before the episode is over, he'll become an Hombre Man and win a spritzing duel with his nemesis, the other Hombre Man.

January 4, 1996:

Joey stars as the king in a play that gets deadly reviews. (Phoebe gives him some constructive criticism: She suggests that he wear underwear onstage, because when he sits on his throne his "royal subjects" are visible.) A depressed Joey thinks about quitting show biz and reveals that he once thought about becoming a veterinarian—"but then I found out you had to stick your hands into cows and stuff." Luckily, he gets his big break: the part of neurosurgeon Drake Ramoray on *Days of Our Lives*. Talent and perseverance really do pay off. (Oh, and so does sleeping with the casting director.)

January 28, 1996:

Joey gets a cameo as a dying virus victim in *Outbreak II: The Virus Takes Manhattan.* When he hams up his scene, his part is changed to that of a *dead* virus victim.

March 21, 1996:

After boasting in *Soap Opera Digest* that he writes his own dialogue, Joey gets written out of *Days of Our Lives* and Dr. Ramoray is sent on a one-way trip down an elevator shaft. His friends try to make him feel better: "Sorry about your death," says Phoebe. "That really sucks."

March 28, 1996:

Joey swallows his pride and auditions for the tiny

part of Cab Driver #2 on *Another World.* He blows his lines and doesn't get it.

May 9, 1996:

Chandler gives Joey a job as an entry-level data processor ("Don't you need experience for that?" wonders Joey). Joey decides to view the job as an acting gig and assumes the role of "Joseph," a married man with two daughters. Not surprisingly, "Joseph" gets on Chandler's nerves once too often.

May 16, 1996:

Joey auditions for a part in a movie directed by Warren Beatty, in which he's required to kiss a guy. He doesn't get it, and Beatty tells him, "Good actor. Bad kisser."

JOEY AT PLAY: A TIMELINE

First Girlfriend:

Lisa DiBatista. Thanks to her, Joey is able to boast that he is "no stranger to the mustache."

September 22, 1994:

Joey—ever the classy guy—hits on Rachel on her wedding day.

October 20, 1994:

Joey decides he wants to get back together with

his ex-girlfriend Angela. He does so by using Monica to lure away Angela's current love interest, Bob.

November 3, 1994:

Joey reveals that he once had sex in the women's room on the second floor of the New York Public Library.

November 17, 1994:

While waiting for the subway, Joey meets a former Macy's colleague: the Obsession Girl. But she sees his VD poster on the wall and gives him the freeze.

December 15, 1994:

During his gig as Santa's helper, Joey meets a hot single mom named Sandy and invites her to spend New Year's Eve with him. She brings her kids along and ends up making out with Max, the science geek, in Monica's bedroom.

January 12, 1995:

Chandler claims that Joey broke the table during his "little breakfast adventure with Angela Delvecchio."

January 19, 1995:

In a touching father-son moment, Joey tells his dad he doesn't know if he's ever been in love. "Then you haven't," says the wise Joey Sr.

February 9, 1995:

Joey finally gets a date with Lorraine, whom he's been chasing for four months. (She can pick up quarters with her toes!)

February 23, 1995:

Joey falls for Ursula, Phoebe's twin sister. He buys her a sweater for her birthday and even takes her to the Ice Capades and the Rainbow Room. He says, "I've never been with a woman before where . . . where I didn't want to screw it up." But then Ursula breaks his heart for no apparent reason. Phoebe pretends to be her sister in order to let him down easy, which results in a big, passionate kiss between the two Friends.

May 11, 1995:

A maternity ward is not your typical pickup scene, but that's where Joey meets Lydia, a Celtics fan and very-soon-to-be-mother. With the real father nowhere in sight, Joey assists in the delivery room and finds himself falling for the new mom. Any possibilities for a romance fade when the real dad finally does show up.

May 18, 1995:

Joey dates Melanie, who runs a fruit-basket business, but he can't have sex with her because he's getting paid to be a subject in a fertility study. Monica clues him in to the fact that he can please Melanie in other ways, and he tries it. "And the response I got! Man, oh, man, it was like a ticker-tape parade!"

September 28, 1995:

While working as the Bijan for Men Guy, Joey asks out a fellow cologne-spritzer named Annabel, but she goes out with the Hombre Man instead—until Joey betters him in a duel.

October 5, 1995:

Joey mentions to his friends that when he first moved to New York he went out with a "really hot, great kisser" who happened to have, "like, the biggest Adam's apple." Hmmm.

November 2, 1995:

Joey and Chandler baby-sit for Ben. They try to use the infant as a babe magnet but fail miserably.

January 4, 1995:

Joey sleeps with a hot casting director in order to get a part on *Days of Our Lives.*

January 28, 1996:

Joey dates his stalker, Erika Ford (Brooke Shields). She sucks his finger over dinner.

May 2, 1996:

Joey announces that he doesn't want Shannon Cooper or Stacey Roth to be invited to Rachel's birthday party because they "steal stuff." This turns out to be guy code. Translation: he slept with them but never called them afterward. After the party, or rather, *parties* (one has Rachel's mom as a guest, the other has her dad), Joey pushes Rachel's mom into a corner and gives her an impressively lengthy kiss. Don't get the wrong idea; he does it only to keep her from seeing Rachel's dad. (Though kissing a friend's mom is technically considered "breaking the code," under these circumstances it's probably forgivable.)

May 16, 1996:

Joey calls up Angela and asks her out, even though she's still going out with "that guy." She hangs up on him. Oh, well. At least he gets to kiss Ross.

FAMILY

Joey says he has six siblings, but sometimes the number changes to seven. That's Joey for you. His father, Joey Senior, is a pipe fitter, and it turns out that his mom, Gloria, was pregnant when she married Joey Senior.

SPECIAL TALENTS

Joey can play "Seasons in the Sun" with his armpit.

Three Embarrassing Facts About Joey

1. He once acted in a porn film, playing the Xerox repair man who couldn't perform his job because two people were performing on the Xerox machine. His line: "You know, that's bad for the paper tray."
2. He spent $3,500 at Porcelain Safari for his "animals," another $1,100 at Everything Lucite, and $2,300 at Isn't It Chrome-antic?
3. He has pet names for his penis. In 1994 he referred to it as "Little Joey." He later refers to it as "the Little General" (he promoted it from "the Little Major" after sleeping with Denise DiMarco).

Three Interesting Facts About Joey

1. He doesn't always wear underwear.
2. He likes to cook in the nude (but nothing that spatters).
3. He holds the Friends' record for intra-Friends kissing, having kissed Chandler (on New Year's Eve 1994), Phoebe (who was disguised as her twin sister), Ross (who kissed him as a favor to prepare for a role), and Phoebe again (she kissed him as a favor, to assess his technique). So how does Joey rate as a kisser? Just fine, says Phoebe: "I'd recommend you to a friend."

	MATT LEBLANC	JOEY TRIBBIANI
Early Experience:	Appeared in commercial for Heinz ketchup	Appeared in commercial for Super Pizza
Modeling:	Posed in Versace and Moschino for Saks men's wear catalog	Posed as poster boy for venereal disease
Other Experience:	Appeared in sexy cable TV show *Red Shoe Diaries*	Appeared in porno film as copier repair-man
First TV Series Role:	Chuck Berder in CBS's *TV 101*	Dr. Drake Ramoray in NBC's *Days of Our Lives*
Roommate:	Lady (a dog)	Chandler

PHOEBE BUFFAY (PLAYED BY LISA KUDROW)

To borrow a point from a theme song you may be familiar with, it really *hasn't* been Phoebe's year. One of her massage clients dies on her table. She gets a great recording deal, then deliberately blows it off (will "Smelly Cat" never get a break?). Her gig at Central Perk is threatened by another musician, a "professional" who claims to know *all* the guitar chords. She gets fired at the kids' library because some parents find her songs inappropriate. Her gay husband turns up, says he's in love, asks for a divorce, then tells her he isn't gay anymore. Her father—or, rather, the guy in the picture frame, who she always *thought* was her father—turns out not to be; he's just one of those generic guys whose photos wind up in picture frames. (Wonder what will happen when she learns that the framed photo of Grandpa is really Albert Einstein?) She runs over her stepmother's dog. She learns that *Old Yeller* doesn't really have a happy ending. And, to top it all off, she gets the chicken pox.

Of course, there is an upside. This year Phoebe got a whole new wardrobe, a whole new hairdo, and a half brother who shed some illumination on their deadbeat dad: Frank Buffay was always happiest when he was walking on stilts.

PHOEBE AT WORK: A TIMELINE

First Employer:

Dairy Queen. Phoebe says she received her first paycheck on a day when there was "a cave-in in one of the mines, and eight people were killed."

Occupation:

By day she's a masseuse (skilled in herbal wraps and shiatsu); by night she's a singer (she performs—free of charge—at Central Perk).

May 4, 1995:

Against his better judgment, Chandler hires Phoebe to temp for his secretary, who's having one breast reduced. (Phoebe needs the work because she foolishly taught all her clients the art of self-massage.)

November 2, 1995:

Phoebe can't believe it when Central Perk replaces her with a "professional" singer. The flabbergasted Phoebe tells Rachel that Central Perk is *her* gig, that it's *her* name written outside in chalk, and, as everyone knows, "you can't just erase . . . chalk."

January 18, 1996:

Bad day at the massage cubicle: An elderly client dies on Phoebe's massage table and sends her restless spirit into Phoebe's body.

January 28, 1996:

Phoebe is thrilled with her new job singing to kids at the library—but the kids' parents are less than thrilled with some of Phoebe's songs, and the cute library guy who hired her now has to fire her.

February 22, 1996:

Phoebe gets discovered! A record producer makes a deal for her to record "Smelly Cat" *and* do a video. Phoebe looks great in the video. She sounds great, too. There's only one problem: The voice singing the song belongs to somebody else.

PHOEBE AT PLAY: A TIMELINE

Marital Status:

Six years ago, Phoebe was secretly married to Duncan, a gay Canadian ice dancer in need of a green card. In October 1995 she agreed to divorce him when he told her he wanted to marry someone else: another woman. A baffled Phoebe asked Duncan how it was possible for him to be straight, since he was funny, smart, and threw "great Academy Award parties."

First Love:

An albino who washed windows near the Port Authority bus station. (Like Phoebe's mother, he ended up committing suicide.)

Before We Met Her:

Phoebe slept with a boyfriend of Monica's just one hour after they broke up. She once went out with a newly divorced man, but the relationship suffered when it turned out that his kids liked *her* more than they liked him. She also had a boyfriend named Randy Brown, but her sister, Ursula, stole him away from her.

October 6, 1994:

Phoebe has a date with a guy who walks her to the subway and says, "We should do this again." The translation, according to Monica, is: "You will never see me naked."

October 20, 1994:

Phoebe dumps a boyfriend named Tony because he's "not fun anymore." She wonders if maybe it has something to do with "his hunger strike."

November 3, 1994:

Phoebe lusts after Paolo: "I just want to bite his bottom lip."

December 15, 1994:

Phoebe admonishes a Central Perk patron for speaking while she's singing. He explains to her that he was just telling his friend that Phoebe is the most beautiful woman he has ever seen. Just as love blossoms, David (Hank Azaria), a scientist, wins a grant to go to Minsk for three years. She urges him to accept it; sadly, he does.

January 5, 1995:

Phoebe falls for Coma Guy and battles Monica for his affection; she decides he must be an artistic soul. When he regains consciousness, she finds out he isn't.

January 19, 1995:

Phoebe briefly dates the annoying, overanalyzing Roger (Fisher Stevens), a shrink all her friends hate but whom she likes because he's not too "shrinky." She dumps him when he puts down her friends for having "a dysfunctional group dynamic."

February 9, 1995:

Phoebe considers going out with Roger again because Valentine's Day is "such a couple-y day." Instead, she hangs out drinking beer with Rachel and Monica. They discuss bad boyfriends, and she brings up Pete the Weeper, who earned his name because he always cried during sex. When the girls build a boyfriend bonfire, she burns a receipt from a dinner date with Nokululeoh. Don't ask.

November 9, 1995:

Phoebe, deep in lust, can't figure out why her new boyfriend, Scott, won't put out. Finally she manages to seduce him by assuring him that he doesn't have to call her afterward if he doesn't want to. Joey is extremely impressed with the guy's technique.

January 28, 1996:

Phoebe hooks up with Rob Donnen (Chris Isaak) when he books her to sing at the children's library, then unhooks when he has to fire her.

May 9, 1996:

Phoebe's all set for two weeks of romance with Ryan (Charlie Sheen), a Navy officer she met long ago in Washington Square Park (he threw saltwater taffy in her case because he had no change). Her plans are thwarted when she comes down with the chicken pox.

FAMILY

Phoebe has a twin sister named Ursula, with whom she's no longer close—despite the fact that they "were one egg once." She also has a brother (whom Ursula mentioned in an episode of *Mad About You*) and a half brother named Carl. Her mother committed suicide when she was fourteen; her stepdad is in prison; her father, Frank Buffay, is a pharmacist who deserted Phoebe's mom *and* his second wife. Phoebe currently lives with her grandmother, Frances, an eccentric cab driver.

Special Talents

Phoebe can sleep in public places. She also makes the world's best oatmeal raisin cookies, but she doesn't prepare them too often because she feels it wouldn't be fair "to the other cookies." And, as we learned in the first episode of the second season, she can cut hair . . . sort of.

Four Embarrassing Facts about Phoebe

1. She was once dumped by a guy because she fell asleep while watching *This Is Spinal Tap.*
2. She has a hard time remembering her phone number, because, as she explains, "I never call me."
3. Milwaukee is the strangest place she's ever had sex.
4. She needs to refer to crib notes when she's driving: "Brake left, gas right."

The Many Moods of Phoebe

Phoebe the Optimist:

Even though she knows that "only once in a blue moon does a dog's ear grow back," Phoebe still holds out hope for the ear of the dog she ran over.

Phoebe the Pessimist:

She thinks *Old Yeller* is a "sick doggie snuff film" and suggests *It's a Wonderful Life* be retitled *It's a Sucky Life,* and *Just When You Think It Can't Suck Any More, It Does.*

Phoebe the Flexible:

Despite the fact that she lost the tweezers to Operation, she keeps the game around, because, she says, "we can still prep the guy."

Phoebe the Curious:

While playing Scrabble, she wonders aloud if *yunt* is a word.

Phoebe the Considerate:

She feels sorry for Chandler and Joey's Foosball players because they're "twenty armless guys joined at the waist by a steel bar, forced to play soccer forever." She comforts Monica's hair before cutting it, promising "none of you will feel a thing."

Phoebe the Giver:

She gives Ross a condom to celebrate his first date in nine years and tells him, "If things don't work out, you can always make a lubricated balloon animal with a little point on its head." When Marcel the monkey departs for San Diego, she gives him a poem and warns him not to eat it until he gets on the plane.

Amy Paulsen

Four Reasons Phoebe Hasn't Hit the Big Time with Her Music

1. The subject of her signature song, "Smelly Cat," has no endearing qualities. Basically, the cat just smells.
2. Her lyrics lean toward the morbid: One night at Central Perk, her set of thirteen songs included twelve about her mom's suicide and one about a snowman (in which her mom's suicide was prominently featured).
3. In addition to foul felines, she also sings about rodents (i.e., rats who play maracas).
4. The songs she sings at the children's library cover the following topics: parents who lie about a grandmother's death; how farm animals get turned into meat; bisexuals who may or may not be deluding themselves.

	Lisa Kudrow	**Phoebe Buffay**
Father:	Famous headache expert	Pharmacist
Education:	B.S. in biology from Vassar; planned to go into medicine	School of Hard Knocks; "expert" in psychic health
Career Setbacks:	Hired to play Roz on *Frasier,*	Hired to play "Smelly Cat" in

	but fired after one day; replaced by Peri Gilpin	music video, but had voice replaced by another singer
Plays:	Pool (expertly)	Guitar (inexpertly)
Love Life:	Recently married to French advertising exec	Formerly married to Canadian ice dancer

2

MARCEL: THE LIFE AND TIMES OF THE SEVENTH FRIEND

On December 15, 1994, a brown capuchin monkey named Marcel captured the hearts of *Friends* viewers across America. The cast of *Friends* was slightly less enchanted. "He ate live worms and vomited," Matthew Perry told *TV Guide*. "It was a little gross."

"I hate the monkey," David Schwimmer told *Entertainment Weekly*. "I wish it were dead."

And so it came as no surprise to insiders that Marcel was shipped off to the San Diego Zoo just four months after he made his first appearance. But though Marcel's time on *Friends* was brief, it was never dull. In one episode alone, he ran away from home, was pursued and shot at by an animal control investigator, and was kidnapped by Mr. Heckles (who put him in a dress and called him "Patty the Monkey").

But the good times came to a screeching halt when

it was determined that the terminally horny Marcel had reached sexual maturity and needed to get away for some "monkey lovin'," leaving Ross—if not David Schwimmer—devastated: "One day he was this little thing, and then before you know it, he's this little thing I can't get off my leg."

Ross spent an entire episode trying to find a good home for his little friend. Disappointed when Marcel wasn't accepted at the Scranton Zoo, he wisely turned down an offer from the very slimy Dr. Baldharar, proprietor of an "interactive wildlife experience." (Ross's suspicions were raised when Baldharar asked whether Marcel could handle a "small blade.") Ultimately Marcel was sent packing—off to the San Diego Zoo, and off the series.

Since then, Marcel has been back for only one guest visit, in the much-hyped "The One After the Super Bowl" episode. Ross, on a business trip in California, stops by the zoo to see Marcel and receives bad news from the zoo administrator: "He got sick. And then he got sicker. And then he got a little better. But then he died." Ross is distraught—until a zookeeper tips him off to the *real* story: Marcel has been sold on the black market and is now working in show biz. Ross tracks him down to the set of *Outbreak II: The Virus Takes Manhattan,* where he is amazed to discover that Marcel has become a big celebrity. (How big? Well, in human terms, they say he's the equivalent of Cybill Shepherd.)

But celebrity hasn't gone to Marcel's head; he

manages to find the time to get together with his old friend, and the two spend a carefree, hand-holding, ice-cream-slurping, silly-grinning afternoon together, montage style. Is there anything so precious as the love between a man and his monkey?

Marcel: The Vital Statistics

Favorite Meal:

Banana cake with mealworms.

Unsuitable Snacks:

Deodorant sticks, bathmats, and Scrabble letters—specifically *M, O,* and *K* ("We think he was trying to spell *monkey,*" says Chandler at the emergency room).

Favorite Toys:

A stuffed animal known as Harry Elephantay, candle wax, the remote control.

Favorite Song:

"The Lion Sleeps Tonight."

Favorite TV Shows:

Jeopardy! and *Entertainment Tonight.*

Nasty Habits:

Poops in shoes and hats; pees on Monica's coffee table.

Stupid Monkey Tricks:

Can retrieve items on command (a proud Ross remarks, "I think he's finally mastered the difference between 'bring me the'. . . and 'pee in the . . . ' "). Can juggle balled-up socks and a melon, according to Chandler. Can put a CD in the player *and* turn it on. Is a terrific dancer. Gets the television stuck in Spanish-language mode.

Objects of His Affection:

Rachel's Barbie doll ("I've got a Malibu Barbie who won't be wearing white to her wedding"). Ross's leg. Rachel's Curious George doll ("Let's just say my Curious George doll is no longer curious"). A lamp. A chair.

TV and Film Credits:

A commercial for Monkeyshine beer, and the movie *Outbreak II: The Virus Takes Manhattan.*

MONKEY BUSINESS

All right. This is complicated, so pay attention: Marcel is a *fictional* capuchin monkey who's played by a real capuchin monkey named Monkey (who, unlike Marcel, is a she, not a he). Now, Monkey has a stand-in monkey named Katie, and both monkeys are represented by an animal rental outfit called Benay's Bird and Animal Rentals. Here's a conversation with Benay Karp, the owner.

TV Guide: Who spent more time playing Marcel, Monkey or Katie?

Benay Karp: Definitely Monkey. Monkey is more highly trained, whereas Katie is more affectionate. Monkey is older; Katie's newer—that's why she doesn't do as many tricks.

TV Guide: Did either monkey develop a close relationship with any of the cast members?

B.K.: Katie established her best relationship with Matt LeBlanc. He was very affectionate with her. He's a real animal lover, I think. He's a really, really nice guy.

TV Guide: Why did the show end up getting rid of the monkey?

B.K.: Politically, I can't say why the monkey isn't on the show. But if you watch any of the interviews with David Schwimmer, that will give you an idea.

TV Guide: How did Monkey and Katie get along with David?

B.K.: It wasn't like they had a clash or anything like that. . . .

TV Guide: When the monkeys came back for the Super Bowl episode, did they remember the cast?

B.K.: People think of them as little people, and they're really not. They're *monkeys.* But because they look so much like us, we put human emotions and characteristics onto them. Really, it's inappropriate. So when they went back on the show, they recognized everybody, but it wasn't as if they ran across the stage and wrapped their little arms around them and said, "Oh, hi, David!" That's not the way they would behave.

TV Guide: Does Monkey really like banana cake with mealworms?

B.K.: Oh, sure! She would love that. Mealworms are her favorite treat.

TV Guide: Is it true she was eating mealworms and vomiting them?

B.K.: I don't think she ever vomited them up. I think these stories just get bigger and bigger. Monkey was really, really good on the show.

TV Guide: Will we see Monkey on the show again?

B.K.: It really kind of depends on the cast. I know David was quoted one time as saying that you can do the most awesome scene in the world, and if the animal doesn't do it right, then they're not going to use that scene. And if the *animal* does it right and *you're* not happy with it, they'll use the one where the animal did it right. It's a great show, everybody on it is unbelievable, but it's a hard show. It's really late hours. If somebody flubs their lines fifty times, nobody hates them, but if the monkey doesn't do it right *once,* then it's the monkey's fault that we're here until one o'clock in the morning.

The show is so popular, with or without Monkey, that I don't know if she'll be back. She might come back for guest appearances. I hope.

TV Guide: Would Monkey make a good pet?

B.K.: No. No. These monkeys are *not* pets. I think in New York you actually can have them as pets, but they shouldn't be. They are exotic animals. They'll poop where they want, they throw their poop, they bite, they smell. But they are good working animals; they're very intelligent.

TV Guide: You've worked with other animals on *Friends,* haven't you?

B.K.: We've had a *lot* of animals on the show. Even Smelly Cat! In the video. Remember? A woman throws the cat out the door, and Phoebe follows the cat down the street. That was a hard one. We had to get that cat to do a lot of stuff. Oh! And we had the attack pigeon! Rachel opened up the window and it followed her all over the house. That was a hard one, too. That was more than one bird. We had one bird that flew in; we had another bird that chased her on the floor. We had another bird that flew up onto the table, and that same bird is the one that read the comics. We had another one that was caught in the pot, and another one that flew out of the pot. That was a *great* one.

3

Friends (and Lovers and Acquaintances) of the Friends

Will there ever be a seventh Friend? One who's not a monkey? In a word, hellno. So to keep us from getting bored with the steadfast six, the producers of the show came up with a clever solution: Guest stars! Lots of 'em! All the time!

Friends guest stars are a lucky lot. They get to have fun names like Rastatter or Baldharar. And they get to do fun things like sing along with Phoebe or stand around with Chandler in an ATM vestibule. And then they get to talk about the experience, which is exactly what some of them are doing right here in thesc exclusive *TV Guide* interviews.

MICHAEL McKEAN played Mr. Rastatter, the Mockolate meister who hired Monica to invent holiday Mockolate recipes. Other credits: played David St. Hubbins in *This Is Spinal Tap* (which he also cowrote) and the Lenny half of Lenny and Squiggy on *Laverne and Shirley.*

TV Guide: What is it like to work on *Friends*?

Michael McKean: You get to look at these three cute girls all week. Four, counting Lauren Tom [who played Ross's girlfriend, Julie]. It was her last week on the show, and she and I have been going out ever since. . . . We wound up hanging out and started seeing each other. I said, "Well, this makes up for the light paycheck, boys."

TV Guide: How did this Rastatter guy come about? Was he created with you in mind?

M.M.: *(Laughing)* I don't think so. I think they just wrote this kind of unctuous, smiley guy with no principles, and mine was the first name that sprang to mind. I seem to have a corner on that character, the amusing rat.

TV Guide: What was Rastatter's actual position at the Mockolate company?

M.M.: He was, I would say, head of marketing—or at least, head of this particular campaign. Just a person who believes in his product because his job is to believe in it. I don't think he really believes in anything.

TV Guide: Do you think a guy with a name like Rastatter is destined to have that kind of job?

M.M.: I don't know. You'll have to talk to my psychiatrist, Dr. Couch.

TV Guide: What other products do you think this company made?

M.M.: I have my own theories. This guy would probably market a cheese-flavored soft drink if he thought it would sell. My father was in advertising for a short time. You walk around with a preoccupied look on your face because you know you have to sell something nobody wants. It is an interesting world, not one I'd like to spend much time in.

TV Guide: We haven't talked about Mockolate yet. What do you suspect the main ingredients are?

M.M.: I would say chalk. On certain boxes of candy that you get at the movies, if it doesn't say the word *chocolate*, it usually says the word *chocolate-y*, which means it's *not* chocolate. There's a certain amount of cocoa that you have to have in it to call it chocolate. So any time you see *chocolate-y* things—"with *chocolate-y* chips!"—you go, "Hmmm! Well, *that's* something that's not made of chocolate!" And these things are always very chalky.

TV Guide: What would account for the bubbles, though? Didn't Mockolate bubble?

M.M.: I think it's all those Pop Rocks factories

that went under. I think they bought a lot of stock in them and stuck a lot of sodium carbonate in there. Otherwise it would just lie in your mouth and not dissolve. It's an aid in predigestion.

TV Guide: What about Fishtachios, that other product your character was trying to sell Monica on?

M.M.: Fishtachios! Apparently there's cat hair in there. Other than that, I don't know what to tell ya.

TV Guide: If you were stranded on a desert island and had to choose between starvation, a bar of Mockolate, or a container of Fishtachios, which would you choose?

M.M.: If there were no saw available so I could remove my foot and eat that, I think that I would probably go for the Mockolate. Mix it with a little coconut milk, it's not that bad.

TV Guide: Have you ever eaten a real-life equivalent of Mockolate?

M.M.: I try not to make a habit of eating too many substandard things. One time, an old girlfriend gave me a little grab bag of candy she bought in Chinatown or someplace. And nothing tasted right. I kept tasting mothballs and petroleum jelly. They didn't even have the ingredients printed on the little cube, so it could have been virtually anything.

TV Guide: The Friends have been known to watch

Laverne and Shirley in Spanish, or rather, *Laverne y Shirley*. Have you ever seen it?

M.M.: Ooh, briefly. The guy who does my voice was not the result of a nationwide talent search. It's kind of like the same guy that does the Mentos commercials. The guy they got for Squiggy, though, is pretty damned close.

HARRY SHEARER played Dr. Baldharar, the unsavory zoo guy who tried to take Marcel off Ross's hands. Other credits: played Derek Smalls in *This Is Spinal Tap* (which he also cowrote) and supplies the voices of Mr. Burns, Smithers, Principal Skinner, and Ned Flanders on *The Simpsons.*

TV Guide: Describe Dr. Baldharar for us.

Harry Shearer: Unscrupulous zoo proprietor. Ross was looking for a place to send the monkey, and I operated a substandard zoo just across the Mexican border. It was a transborder situation.

TV Guide: What were you planning to do with that monkey?

H.S.: I think there was some exploitation-type spectacle involved. Probably something along the lines of Mexican gladiators.

TV Guide: Have you worked with monkeys before?

H.S.: I believe this was the first monkey I have

worked with in my show business career. The monkey entered late in the scene. I believe there was more than one. I think they had, like, backup monkeys. And at this point everyone was fairly expert on the personality differences between the two monkeys. I took their word for it that the one working that day was the nicer of the bunch. I figured, "Okay, I'm not going to test this."

TV Guide: What were your interactions with the monkey outside of the scene?

H.S.: None. The minute the rehearsals of the scenes were over, the monkey was whisked, I guess, to a very luxurious monkey trailer somewhere on the set. A Monkey-bago.

TV Guide: The cast is said to have hated the monkeys. Did you get a sense of that?

H.S.: Well, I don't know any cast of any show or any movie that likes monkeys. Because any time a monkey is on the screen, that's what people are going to be looking at. No actor in his right mind likes monkeys as costars.

TV Guide: So I guess you were doing everybody a favor, trying to get Marcel out of there.

H.S.: Yeah—I was part of the process of retrieving the sanity of the cast from monkey envy.

TV Guide: Do you have any plans to return and maybe kidnap Marcel?

H.S.: When you ask an actor if he has plans to return to the show, it's like asking somebody if they're going to win the lottery. It's not in my hands. But I would, of course. One of the producers, Kevin Bright, is an old friend of mine, and we do things for each other on a fairly consistent basis. So if Kevin asks me, of course I'll do it.

TV Guide: A guy once dumped Phoebe because she fell asleep during *Spinal Tap.* Is that possible in the real world?

H.S.: If they're watching on home video and have not got the sound at the properly excessively loud level, I guess it's theoretically possible, but that's not the recommended exhibition procedure. The recommended procedure is you watch it with the sound on so loud you can't possibly fall asleep. So that would be a tech support question.

TV Guide: Any other pointers on the ideal viewing of the movie?

H.S.: Ideal is to get about five hundred young white males with long hair to stand there shaking their heads all around you while you're watching. Preferably tattooed.

TV Guide: Considering that Phoebe actually did fall asleep, do you think that's grounds for dismissal?

H.S.: Yeah! I think in the pantheon of reasons to dump somebody, that's pretty high on the list.

JILL CONNICK played herself (using her maiden name, Jill Goodacre), the Victoria's Secret model, who got stuck with Chandler in an ATM vestibule.

TV Guide: You gave Chandler his first TV kiss. What was it like?

Jill Connick: It was awesome because he is so sweet. I would love to be on the show again.

TV Guide: Have you ever offered gum to a stranger before?

J.C.: Always, at the checkout counter in the grocery store.

TV Guide: Do you think Chandler's response to the offer—"Gum would be perfection"—is a good pickup line?

J.C.: It's definitely the most *unusual* pickup line. It's perfect for Chandler.

TV Guide: Any advice on how Chandler might be more successful with women?

J.C.: Have me back on the show, and I'll show you!

TV Guide: Have you ever gotten a guy so tongue-tied that he couldn't even talk to you?

J.C.: Harry [Connick, her husband]. When we met he just sort of stuttered . . . it was quite funny.

TV Guide: Which Friend would you most like to be stuck with in an ATM vestibule?

J.C.: Chandler again . . . anytime!

PETER DELUISE played one of the two bullies who picked a fight with Ross and Chandler at Central Perk. Other credits: played Doug Penhall on *21 Jump Street.*

TV Guide: How did you come to play the bully?

Peter Deluise: I got on the standard way—I auditioned and got the part. I think I got it because I'm not *completely* anonymous and I'm physically imposing. And I may have been funny during the auditioning process.

TV Guide: Why was your character picking on Ross and Chandler?

P.D.: Well, they were sitting on the couch! Then they started to get smart with us. I guess I didn't appreciate that very much.

TV Guide: In real life, are you someone who bullies people or gets bullied?

P.D.: I'm definitely a bully. Oh, sure. I have two younger brothers, and I'm definitely a bully in that respect. I used to torment my brothers when I was younger. And I still torment them to this day.

TV Guide: Can you rank the three guy characters on the show in terms of wimpiness?

P.D.: Well, Ross is the most sensitive character, so he's most likely to be put upon physically. And I think Chandler is more likely to come back with a cutting remark, so he'd be able to defend himself in that way. So I would put him second. And then Joey is much more physically imposing and he relies a little bit more on his physicality to defend himself. So I think he'd be hardest to bully.

TV Guide: He's scrappy.

P.D.: Yeah, if he was at a loss for words, he certainly wouldn't be at a loss to throw a punch.

TV Guide: You didn't actually come to blows with them, but you would have kicked their butts, right?

P.D.: I doubt it. You know, I think that we had so much bad karma by that time that some higher power would have made sure we lost the fight. They would have won, somehow. In the end, bullies always get theirs.

CHRISSIE HYNDE played Stephanie, the professional singer hired to replace Phoebe at Central Perk. Other credits: is lead singer of The Pretenders.

TV Guide: Have you ever played in a coffeehouse setting like Central Perk?

Chrissie Hynde: Many years ago, in Mexico.

TV Guide: Would you rather play in a coffeehouse or a stadium?

C.H.: A stadium—simply because I would rather play with my band, and they wouldn't fit in a coffeehouse.

TV Guide: What advice would you give to Phoebe, the aspiring singer-songwriter?

C.H.: Hang in there. Your number will come up eventually.

TV Guide: What do you think of "Smelly Cat"? Would you ever consider performing it?

C.H.: It seems to have struck a chord with the general public, but I *personally* don't think I can do the song justice.

TV Guide: Which of your own songs is as obscure and yet personal to you as "Smelly Cat" is to Phoebe?

C.H.: "I'm a Mother" [from the album *Last of the Independents*].

JON LOVITZ played Steve, the stoned guy who fails to appreciate Monica's fine cooking during a chef audition. Other credits: was a regular on *Saturday Night Live* from 1985 to 1990 and currently stars (with his voice only) in *The Critic* on Comedy Central.

TV Guide: What made you decide to be a guest on *Friends*?

Jon Lovitz: I grew up with Lisa Kudrow. She's like my sister. And Courteney Cox and I worked together on this movie, *Mr. Destiny,* about six years ago, so we became really good friends. So they called me up to do the show. The show wasn't a big hit the way it is now. I read it and thought it was funny, and I thought it would be fun to work with them. By the time the show came out, it had become this *huge* hit. So I went in thinking I'd do them a favor, but as it turns out, they were doing me a favor. I'm kind of proud. I was, like, their first guest star.

TV Guide: Your character had one line that struck us as really funny. . . .

J.L.: "Smack my ass and call me Judy?" The writers thought of that. I thought it was hysterical.

TV Guide: How has the show managed to be so consistently funny?

J.V.: They write the show really well, and they picked the perfect cast. Everybody is really funny, and they work well together. It's chemistry with these things. You never know.

ROMANTIC FRIENDS OF THE FRIENDS

COSIMO FUSCO played Paolo, Rachel's Italian lover.

TV Guide: Your character has made passes at both Rachel and Phoebe. Which of the women do you think he'd most like to spend an evening with?

Cosimo Fusco: There is no doubt: Rachel is my girl—is *his* girl. Yes. He is a stranger to this world, and all these people are very new to him. But Rachel, she could be Italian. Phoebe looks too Anglo-Saxon to him, you know what I mean? Phoebe is very scary for him. The reason I—I mean *he*—made a move on her is he just can't help it. He's in love with life. Phoebe is a very attractive lady as well. And she was right there, and, oh, God! It was crazy! To get in trouble . . .

TV Guide: Do you think Paolo is the right guy for Rachel?

C.F.: I think he would be, he could be, if they gave him more chances to grow. He can't seem to get around the language barrier. But he really does like Rachel. He just has this block in communication. He doesn't know her really well and he can't feel for her too much if they can't communicate.

TV Guide: Would Paolo fight Ross for her?

C.F.: Of course! With a sword and a horse and everything. He's a real cavalier.

TV Guide: Do you think Ross could be the right guy for Rachel?

C.F.: I should say not! It's a bit of a stretch, not just because I'm talking from Paolo's side. Rachel needs more excitement, more . . . edgier stuff. She should be in a bit of trouble. I think Ross gives her too much security.

TV Guide: If you could be any of the guy characters, which would you be?

C.F.: Chandler. In a way, I have his kind of rhythm, his kind of understanding in life. But I haven't expressed it yet in the show because I'm not playing that kind of guy. But it would be funny if Paolo turns into some kind of fast-talker. Because he's actually from the same sort of street-smart background, but from another country. He is very fast and funny.

TV Guide: What do you think Paolo's life is like?

C.F.: I had to make up my mind and give him some kind of a life because I wasn't given one. I figure he's the Dr. Jekyll–Mr. Hyde kind of a guy. He might have a serious relationship going in Italy, but it's not really happening. He's in America for work reasons. I made up my mind and *his* mind for the character to be into fashion.

TV Guide: What's his apartment like?

C.F.: Actually, the apartment in New York is nothing to him because he doesn't even know where he is. He spends part of the time there and then he's back to Rome. I think he has the essential stuff: lots of clothes, some good music, some good *entertaining,* you know, atmosphere for his victims, if you know what I mean. Ha, ha, ha! And good alcohol! But he's not as slimy as he looks. He's a good guy. He means well. He's not a dangerous guy.

TV Guide: If he's a good guy, why did he break Rachel's heart?

C.F.: You know what? He's one of those guys who's sort of afraid of the word *marriage.* You don't have to go far to find that kind of man. But I think he's resisted the idea of liking this girl or *any* girl to that extent. He's in that stage of life. But it's not Rachel. Once he makes up his mind and maybe decides to move to the States, who knows?

TV Guide: If they asked you to be the seventh Friend, would you?

C.F.: Of course, with pleasure, with love. It was great for me, because I was there when they were filming show number four. I feel like part of the family. I've seen them cry when the show was picked up, it was great. I feel like part of the team. If they even called me for one day here, one day there, I'm there.

MAGGIE WHEELER plays Janice, Chandler's on-again, mostly off-again girlfriend.

TV Guide: Janice is fundamentally a very annoying

person. What is it that endears her so much to the viewers?

Maggie Wheeler: You know, I don't know if I know the answer to that question. I think it's one of the great mysteries of life *(laughs).* Maybe it's her indomitable spirit.

TV Guide: Why is Chandler attracted to her?

M.W.: Well, in the episode when I was pregnant, he said that she's beautiful and smart and she loves him—and so she may not be everybody's cup of tea, but she understands him and she loves him, and it feels good to be at the other end of that. So I think that he's continuously drawn back to it.

TV Guide: And what about Janice's attraction to Chandler?

M.W.: Well, Chandler's fabulous! He's so much fun. He's smart, he's funny, he's sexy. She loves his weaknesses. She sees all of his potential to be happy, and she feels that she's the person who can take him to that place.

TV Guide: Why do you suppose Chandler keeps going back to her?

M.W.: Because when somebody sees your potential, it's very compelling.

TV Guide: What do you say to all those rumors that Chandler is gay?

M.W.: *(In her Janice voice)* Oh, honey, he's not gay. I'm so sure!

TV Guide: We last saw Janice at the season ender, when it turned out that she was Chandler's cyberspace soul mate. Is there a chance she'll be back in the fall?

M.W.: Yes, there is an absolute chance. She'll be ba-aa-ckkk. . . .

LAUREN TOM played Julie, Ross's pre-Rachel girlfriend.

TV Guide: Describe Julie for us.

Lauren Tom: I was just a really nice gal—but Rachel still called me a bitch, because she was jealous. The way that Marta [Kauffman, creator and executive producer] explained it to me was that if it weren't for Rachel, Julie and Ross would probably end up being a couple and staying a couple; that there was nothing really wrong with me except that I wasn't Rachel. It's funny, because when I was first asked to be on the show, they explained the whole arc of the story line, and what would happen, and that it was more to just stall out Rachel and Ross getting together. And I said, "That's okay!" But when the time came, I swear to God, it felt like he was breaking up with *me.*

TV Guide: Do you think Ross and Julie made a good pair?

L.T.: Oh, yeah. I think they would have been fine. It's just that Ross and Rachel had such a history. Like, he had a crush on her for ten years. But I liked the fact that being an Asian-American actress and all, they didn't make any mention of my ethnicity. I didn't speak with an accent. I was just a nice gal.

TV Guide: You were supposed to be from New York, right?

L.T.: I actually pitched that joke to them about Rachel going, "Welcome to my country!" That actually happened to me in New York once. I was trying to buy a soda from one of the hot dog vendors on the street, and he started *talking really loud!* Like, *Do you want a Coke?* And it was like, oh, please.

TV Guide: How did it feel to be the "other woman"?

L.T.: It was hard, because the people who were rooting for Rachel and Ross didn't want me in the picture. A couple of times, some audience members hissed when I kissed Ross. It had nothing to do with *me,* but it was still hard. Then the writers tried to make me feel better because they said that on the Internet there was an "I Love Julie" club. This one person wrote, like, a nine-page journal as if it was Julie's diary. It was creepy.

TV Guide: What was in the journal?

L.T.: It was pretty general. It was just, like, "Well,

PRINCESS

today I went here, and I was thinking about Ross. . . ." Kind of mundane.

TV Guide: But doing the show was a good experience. . . .

L.T.: Last summer I was watching the show at home, and I was, like, "God, is this a good show. I would love to be on this show." And then David Schwimmer, I thought, "Wow, he's so cute, and so funny, I would love to be acting with him!" Honest to God, the next week my agents called and said, "The producers from *Friends* called and wanted to know if you'd do six episodes with them. I was, like, "You call them back right now and tell them yes!"

TV Guide: You didn't get a breakup scene with Ross, did you?

L.T.: They actually wrote one, but they said that the problem with it was that you felt too much sympathy for Julie. So they said, "Our hearts were more with you, and they need to be more with Rachel and Ross." But then they added one more episode just to give me a happy ending.

TV Guide: And this is Russ. Did you see much of a difference between Ross and Russ?

L.T.: You know that he had a fake chin and a fake nose on, right? Fake hair. Still, a person's spirit comes through their eyes. David Schwimmer is such a love. He is just adorable.

TV Guide: Do you find it hard to root for Ross and Rachel now?

L.T.: It's like in real life. You don't want to wish ill will on anyone. I don't think they should break up. I do think it was fun, though, to keep them apart as long as possible. I think they actually could've strung it along even more.

TV Guide: What was it like, coming into such a tightly knit group for six episodes?

L.T.: I felt bad—I don't know if you knew, but the *National Enquirer* printed a huge article that I got fired because I was a bitch. It hurt me so much because there wasn't an ounce of truth in it. I was contracted for six episodes. But they made it seem like the cast didn't like me and had me fired. I never read that paper, but after that happened I started to glance at it in the grocery store, and they did the same thing to Jennifer and to Lisa and to Courteney, trying to paint them as bitches, making them prima donnas, and it's not true. This is the loveliest cast I've ever worked with. They're so close to each other. Maybe they just wanted to write more articles about *Friends.* It's infuriating, though.

TV Guide: It must have been weird for you, though, coming onto a show where everyone else is already friends.

L.T.: It wasn't weird, it was scary. It was like transferring to a new high school. I didn't know anybody, and they were all *so* close. But I have to say, the first day of rehearsal was my birthday and they found out and all took me out to lunch, and it was so sweet. And we would all hang out in Courteney's dressing room. They were very welcoming to me.

TV Guide: If you had your choice, which of the male Friends would you most like to date?

L.T.: Of the men, Matt LeBlanc's character would scare me too much. I think I'm too insecure to go out with a man who's better-looking than me, or who's gone out with so many women. That's not what I'm looking for. Chandler is hysterical, but I think he'd be too hard to get to know. Ross is a warm, sensitive, real man that you can be yourself with. So I'll go with Bachelor Number Three.

CHRIS ISAAK played Rob Donnen, who wooed Phoebe and signed her up to play her songs for kids in a library. Other credits: His albums include *Heart-Shaped World* and *Forever Blue,* and he has had acting roles in *Silence of the Lambs* and *Little Buddha.*

TV Guide: Why didn't you sing in the episode?

Chris Isaak: Well, I guess I didn't see the episode, because I did sing. We sang about some cat.

TV Guide: You sang "Smelly Cat"?

C.I.: Yeah, at the end of the show we sang that

song. I don't know what they did with it. But I played along. Miss Kudrow taught it to me. She handles all my theatrical singing assignments.

TV Guide: What was the best part of working on the star-studded Super Bowl episode?

C.I.: You know the guy from the *Mod Squad*? Linc [Clarence Williams III]? He was on that episode. So to me that was exciting. Brooke Shields was hanging out backstage. She's very savvy and funny, so that was fun. Somebody [in the crew] had a Brooke Shields doll and asked her to sign it. To me that was a sign that I was working with the elite of show business.

TV Guide: How did you get along with Lisa Kudrow?

C.I.: She was very helpful. She helped me with my acting. She said, "Chris, don't look at the lens." You know, you walk onto a set like that, these people have been doing it every day for a couple of years, so you don't know—are they going to be friendly? Are they going to be not so friendly? You don't know if they're going to like each other, let alone you. But she was very nice. She said, "Do you want to go over your lines?" I said, "Over and over my lines!"

TV Guide: Did you get to jam with her?

C.I.: We actually did. We hung out backstage and we did start playing guitar back there. In fact, I ended up hooking her up with my buddies who make guitars. She ended up getting some guitars out of the deal.

TV Guide: What kind?

C.I.: Gibson. A big acoustic guitar. Because she had some kind of funky guitar she was playing. She said *(mimicking Phoebe),* "I'm having trouble playing this," and I picked it up and said, "Yeah, so am I!"

TV Guide: How's her playing?

C.I.: As I said two or three times to different interviewers, she has training in Spanish classical guitar. For the TV show it's very difficult for her to make it look difficult to play those chords. Now, this is all a lie, but I do like the story. Really, though, she's a guitar player like I am. She just wails away on it. No training.

TV Guide: Your character got Phoebe to play for kids. How would her brutally honest songs go over in real life?

C.I.: I think kids don't have any interest in those things. Their minds are focused on more important things: "What's for lunch? Look at those flowers, they look nice." Sometimes adults feel a necessity to explain the things they're interested in to kids: "I want to explain to you about sexuality." "I don't care about it! Can I go play tetherball?"

TV Guide: Have you ever played to kids?

C.I.: I have. They're a tough audience. They can spot you in a second. I played one time on a Christmas kind of TV special with a bunch of little kids around. I was kidding around, being sarcastic, and I said, "This is a song about the time Santa got real sick and almost died." I started to play and I looked over and saw this kid who was looking at me like this was the truth. I thought, "Chris, you've been hanging around with the band too long." I stopped the song and I said, "That was a bad joke. Santa's not sick. Santa's okay." Sarcasm and double entrendre and sophisticated humor don't work on kids. [Considering] Or on the band . . .

TV Guide: What's the most offbeat place you ever played?

C.I.: I played mental institutions. And I've played old folks' homes. You find out that every crowd is different. Like at the institution, I was playing this ballad. With most audiences, they'll wait until the end of the song and if they like it, they'll applaud. Well, right in the middle of the ballad, this guy stands up with tears in his eyes and just starts clapping. Like, "This *moves* me. *Right now* this moves me, and I'm going to clap *right now.*" And I just went, "This is cool."

TV Guide: Have you kept in touch with the cast?

C.I.: I saw Lisa Kudrow again. We presented

something at the Grammys. She's very nice; she doesn't have a big head. When you have to work with these people, you think, "It could be scary. They could be off the deep end, thinking they're Napoleon." But she's right off *Father Knows Best.*

TV Guide: What advice do you have for Phoebe, a struggling singer-songwriter?

C.I.: If there was a real offbeat folk singer like that, probably MTV and VH1 would be battling it out to get her on, to give her a show. The ones who are really sad are the ones who try to do exactly what they've seen on TV five years ago, because they think that's the way to make it. They're always relegated to playing somebody else's music at a bar and wondering, "Why can't I ever break in?" But people who are kind of oblivious to the whole business, half the time that's who they sign up. So I think she would have a big career ahead of her.

4

CHANNEL-SURFING WITH THE FRIENDS

There are those who think the Friends are nothing more than a bunch of coffeehouse slackers, with thoughts no deeper than the foam on their cappuccinos.

But that assessment is simply unfair. As anyone who watches the show knows, the Friends have a rich and varied cultural life. They go to the theater (*Freud!*—the musical), they attend concerts (Hootie & the Blowfish), they read books (*Be Your Own Windkeeper*), and they visit museums (the American Museum of Natural History, where Ross and Rachel consummated their relationship). And no matter how busy they may be, they always find the time to watch TV.

Television is the art that inspires them, consoles them, and transforms them. Without TV their lives would make no sense. (In fact, without TV, they wouldn't even be here.) Here is a sampling of the programming that has shaped their lives.

Baywatch

Chandler and Joey have their own special name for their favorite show: they call it "the Watch." When Joey moves out, the *Baywatch* buddies hook up by phone so they can discuss the finer points as they watch. Chandler: "This is the brilliance of the show: always keep them running. . . . Run, Yasmine, run like the wind!"

The Business Channel

Monica gets addicted to the sight of her initials as they flash by on the cable channel's stock ticker, and ultimately she invests in "her" stock. She actually makes money on it by sticking to her motto: "Get out before they go down." (To which Joey responds, "That is *so* not my motto.") But she loses when she invests in CHP and ZXY.

Days of Our Lives

The Friends follow Joey's progress as Dr. Drake Ramoray, all the way to his bitter end down an elevator shaft.

Entertainment Tonight

Ross tries to get Marcel to watch *Entertainment Tonight* in order to keep the mischievous monkey away from his date, Celia.

Family Matters

Marcel plays with the remote and gets the TV stuck on Spanish-language mode. As they watch *Family Matters,* Rachel says, "Cool. Urkel in Spanish is Urkel." Other dubbed shows include *Laverne y Shirley* (the opening credits go like so: "Cinco, seis, siete, ocho! Schlemiel! Schlamazel!"), *La Connection de Amore (Love Connection), The Waltons,* and *The Patty Duke Show.* (Ross wonders whether it's Patty or Cathy who "enjoys a crepe Suzette.")

Happy Days

Rachel, newly escaped from her wedding ceremony, watches with the girls and comments on the fundamental difference between her and her ex-fiancé and Joanie and Chachi: "See, but Joanie *loved* Chachi. *That's* the difference."

Infomercials

Phoebe and Monica pretend to watch an infomercial for an ultra-absorbent mop, but what they're *really* watching is Rachel and Paolo breaking up on the terrace. (Well, maybe Monica is paying a *little* attention to the infomercial.)

Joey's Porn Movie

The group (plus Julie, minus Phoebe) checks out Joey in the one film credit he doesn't like to include on his résumé.

Lamb Chop's Playalong

Chandler, suffering from nicotine withdrawal, watches with Ross, Rachel, and Phoebe and grumbles, "How old is that sock? If I had a sock on my hand for thirty years, it'd be talking, too."

Monkeyshine Beer Commercial

The Friends notice that the monkey in the Monkeyshine commercial looks just like Marcel. It is. Why would anyone drink Monkeyshine beer? "'Cause it's a jungle out there." Of course.

Phoebe's Video Medley

Phoebe learns that, contrary to what her mom led her to believe, all movies don't have happy endings. After watching *Old Yeller, It's a Wonderful Life, Pride of the Yankees, E.T., Rocky,* and *Charlotte's Web,* she cries, "What kind of world do we live in? E.T. leaves! Rocky loses! Charlotte dies!"

Predators of the Serengeti

Ross and Monica argue over what to watch. Ross wants *Predators,* but Monica has her heart set on *Entertainment Tonight.* In the same episode, Ross makes a TV reference during a phone call, arguing that "if Dino was a velociraptor, he would've *eaten* the Flintstones!"

Public Access

Joey watches a rabbi playing electric guitar because he can't find the remote.

Rachel and Monica's Prom Video

You've got to see it to believe it. Rachel's nose was bigger, and Monica's . . . well, *all* of Monica was bigger. Monica explains it this way: "The camera adds ten pounds." To which Chandler reacts: "So then how many cameras were actually on you?"

Three's Company

As Chandler, Joey, and Phoebe watch, Chandler remarks, "I think this is the episode of *Three's Company* where there's some kind of misunderstanding."

The Tonight Show with Jay Leno

The gang and Paolo watch Chandler's mom, who's on Leno to promote her new book *Euphoria Unbound.* As they watch, Chandler complains that he would rather be watching *Weekend at Bernie's.* Among the details Mrs. Bing shares with America are that she was recently arrested; she craves kung pao chicken after sex; and she once purchased condoms for a young Chandler.

Unnamed Soap Opera

Rachel and Marcel watch, and Rachel provides the monkey with running commentary: "The one with the eye patch is Dr. Frances. He used to be a woman. And that's Raven. We hate her. We're glad she's dying."

SPORTS

Basketball

Joey watches a Knicks game at the hospital while waiting for baby Ben to be born.

Football

During a funeral, Joey surreptitiously watches a New York Giants football game on his Watchman. (A suspicious Chandler says, "Your topcoat just sounded remarkably like Brent Musburger.")

Lumberjack Competition

As burly he-men toss trees, Ross's belief in the theory of evolution is shaken.

Spanish Midget Wrestling

Chandler and Joey are engrossed in a wrestling match when Ross walks in and says he misses Julie. Chandler tries to find the connection: "Spanish midgets . . . Spanish midgets wrestling . . . Julie. Okay, I see how you got there."

Tennis

The Geller family watches a Steffi Graf tennis match, and Mr. Geller admires Steffi's "tush."

THE FAMOUS JOEY AND CHANDLER TV MARATHON

Joey celebrates his *Days of Our Lives* gig by buying a jumbo-screen TV and twin recliner chairs—one for himself and one for Chandler ("Now we can watch *Green Acres* the way it was *meant* to be seen," says an excited Chandler). The boys turn on the set, sink into their seats, and fall into a profound vegetative state, refusing to drink liquids for fear they might have to get up to use the bathroom. The marathon kicks off with *The Dick Van Dyke Show*. ("Rose Marie really belongs on a smaller screen, doesn't she?" Monica remarks.) Joey and Chandler spend the rest of the *Friends* episode enjoying such gems as *Xanadu* and an infomercial for a "miracle car wax." And when a fire alarm goes off in the middle of *Beavis and Butt-head*, the boys *still* don't budge.

THE GAMES FRIENDS PLAY

Boggle
Poker
Trouble
Kerplunk
Twister
Pictionary
Scrabble
Foosball
Monopoly

5

Ross and Rachel: Anatomy of a Romance

It was destiny that kept them apart. And it was destiny that brought them together. No. Wait. It was *Ross* who kept them apart (he was too much of a wuss to ever tell Rachel he loved her). And it was *Chandler* who brought them together (he spilled the beans and ignited Rachel's passion). Poor, sweet, *pathetic* Ross. If it were up to him, Rachel probably *still* wouldn't have a clue. But that's just how we liked it in the first season. Ross's pain was our pleasure. As he pined, Rachel Paolo'd. Then, in season two, the equation was turned upside down, and a new obstacle—that bitch, Julie (Rachel's words, not ours)—was thrown into the course of true love. And then . . . well, here's how it all evolved, from the beginning. . . .

September 22, 1994, the pilot:

In the series pilot, Ross displays what we'll soon recognize to be uncharacteristic boldness: He asks

Rachel if it would be okay if he asked her out sometime. She tells him yes (actually, it's more of a maybe).

September 29, 1994, "The One with the Sonogram at the End":

A sweet foreshadowing of what is to come. Rachel has the jitters because she's about to return her ring to her ex-fiancé, Mr. Potato Head, oops, make that Barry. "When did it get so complicated?" she asks Ross. "Remember back in high school? Didn't you think you were just going to meet someone and fall in love and that'd be it?" "Yeah," Ross said. "I did." The significance of the remark is lost on Rachel.

October 20, 1994, "The One with the East German Laundry Detergent":

Ross invites himself to help Rachel do laundry (which Chandler insists is a date). At the Launderama, he realizes she is a "laundry virgin," which gives him the opportunity to show that he is both sweet *and* domestic. He even shares his Uberweiss laundry detergent (which, unlike Ross, is "extra tough"). Rachel screws up her laundry but manages to face down Horrible Woman who tries to steal her laundry cart. Elated, she kisses Ross, who in turn slams his kisser right into a dryer door.

November 3, 1994, "The One with the Blackout":

Joey warns a lovelorn Ross that he's setting himself up for a fall with Rachel: "You waited too long to make your move and now you're in the Friend Zone." Undaunted, Ross tries to break out of the zone, but is foiled by a pesky feline who interrupts him when he's on the verge of opening his heart to Rachel. To add insult to injury, it turns out the cat belongs to Paolo, a studly Italian neighbor who immediately sweeps Rachel off her feet. Ross gets his digs in by telling Paolo—whose command of the English language is shaky—that he is a "crap weasel."

November 10, 1994, "The One Wherc Nana Dies Twice":

Ross, who's stoned on the four painkillers his mother gave him to calm a muscle spasm, says to Rachel, "I *do* love you. . . . No, I mean it. I *really* love you. . . . I love you . . . the most." She chalks it up to drug-induced ramblings.

January 5, 1995, "The One with Mrs. Bing":

Chandler's mom, the romance novelist, takes one look at Ross and realizes he's got it bad for Rachel (and that he's got it in for Paolo). "The guy's a secondary character; a complication you eventually kill off," she tells Ross. "You know who our hero is? It's you." And then she plants one on him.

January 12, 1995, "The One with the Dozen Lasagnas":

Rachel learns that Paolo is, in fact, a crap weasel. Ross tells her, "You deserve so much better than him. You should be with a guy who knows what he has when he has you." But his words don't have the desired effect: Rachel informs him that she's sick of guys. "I don't even want to think about another guy."

February 9, 1995, "The One with the Candy Hearts":

Chandler urges Ross to ask out another woman, pointing out the obvious: "The Rachel thing's not working; your ex-wife is a lesbian."

March 2, 1995, "The One with All the Poker":

In the middle of a nasty, heated game of poker, Rachel gets a phone call and finds out that her dream job at Saks has been offered to someone else. Instead of quitting, she insists that the game go on and starts a huge betting war with Ross (using big bucks she doesn't have). When she shows her cards—a full house—Ross concedes. As the guys console him, he quietly points out how happy Rachel looks. The guys, suspecting that he let her win, lunge for his cards.

March 9, 1995, "The One Where the Monkey Gets Away":

Hitting on the baby-sitter is always a bad idea—unless you're Ross and the baby-sitter is Rachel (and the baby is a monkey). But when Rachel misplaces Marcel, the evening goes from romantic to frantic. While the unhappy twosome search for the monkey, Ross berates his beloved: "You're just in Rachel-land doing your Rachel thing—totally oblivious to people's monkeys or . . . or people's feelings!" But he apologizes later, and just when he's about to reveal that he cares, Barry walks in and declares his love for her. "We have *got* to start locking that door," says a weary Ross, to no one in particular.

May 4, 1995, "The One with the Ick Factor":

Rachel has sexual dreams about all the guys—except Ross. At least, not until the end of the episode, when Ross catches a napping Rachel murmuring his name. He sits beside her, and she awakens, saying, "We were just . . . Wow . . ." to his loving glance. But before they can make the dream come true, his beeper beeps: Ross is about to become a dad.

May 18, 1995, "The One Where Rachel Finds Out":

It's Rachel's birthday, and Ross can't come to the party (he's leaving for a business trip to China), but he sends along his present: an antique cameo pin she wanted. No one can believe he bought her something so sweet—and so expensive. Except for Chandler, that is, who lets slip the truth. Rachel can't believe it. "I mean, my first night in the city, he mentioned maybe asking me out," she says. "But then nothing ever happened." She can't wait a week to talk to him, so she rushes to the airport—only wouldn't you know it?—she misses him. In the next week she cools to the idea, but then, in the middle of a date, she can't stop fantasizing about Ross. She rushes to the airport, not knowing that Ross is approaching the gate with another woman—one he's kissing, one who's calling him "sweetie."

September 21, 1995, "The One with Ross's New Girlfriend":

Oh, tragedy! Rachel looks on in horror as Ross walks off the plane holding hands with his new girlfriend, Julie. Rachel mopes around the apartment for a while, then has a fling with Paolo. When Ross sees the two together, he tells Rachel she can do a lot better than Paolo and that she should be with someone who will make her as happy as he is with Julie. This advice does *not* cheer her up.

October 12, 1995, "The One with Phoebe's Husband":

Ross makes a confession to Rachel: He and Julie haven't done it yet. As Rachel assimilates this good news, she tells Ross that Julie will find it *really sexy* if he holds out even longer. Ross, no fool, ignores her advice, and on the night that he plans to consummate his new relationship, Rachel does her best to postpone the inevitable. Eventually she accepts the fact that *it will happen,* and even describes to Ross how she'd want it to be if he were seducing *her:* "I'd want you to look really far into my eyes and kiss me in a way that lets me know something amazing is about to happen." And just when we think that something amazing really *is* about to happen between these two, Ross breaks away—and goes back to Julie.

November 9, 1995, "The One Where Ross Finds Out":

In a drunken frenzy, Rachel leaves a message on Ross's machine saying she's over him. The next morning, her memory of the night before is a blank—until Ross stops by and uses her phone to check his messages. "You're over me?" Ross asks. "When . . . when . . . when were you *under* me?" Finally, the truth is revealed—but it's too late, because Ross is with Julie now. Or is it too late? At the end of the day, Ross goes to Central Perk and has a big blowout with Rachel. He leaves. She collapses. He comes back. They kiss, big time. This should have been called "The One We've All Been Waiting For."

November 16, 1995, "The One with The List":

Ross needs to make a decision: Rachel or Julie. Chandler suggests he make a list of each woman's pros and cons. Bad idea. Though Rachel doesn't fare too well on the list (she's spoiled, ditzy, too into her looks, and just a waitress, to name a few cons), Ross decides to go with her because Julie's big fault is unredeemable: "She's not Rachel." Ross rushes to dump Julie. Then Rachel sees the list—and dumps Ross.

December 14, 1995, "The One with Phoebe's Dad":

Ross tries to endear himself to Rachel by giving her a Slinky for Christmas. It doesn't work. He urges her to make a list about *him*, and she does: He's whiny, obsessive, insecure, gutless, and has too much gel in his hair.

January 4, 1996, "The One with Russ":

Rachel starts dating another man: Russ, who looks and sounds and behaves exactly like Ross (a fact that is completely lost on Rachel, Ross *and*

Russ). Once Rachel does see the similarities, she's totally grossed out. She dumps Russ—who then runs into Julie at Central Perk. Their eyes meet, and . . .

February 1, 1996, "The One with the Prom Video":

Rachel still hates Ross, even when he informs her that she's his "lobster" (According to Phoebe, lobsters mate for life). But then something magical happens as the Friends watch a videotape of Monica and Rachel getting ready for their high school prom. In it, they see a geeky young Ross who's so in love with Rachel that he excitedly tries to come to her rescue when it looks like her date is a no-show. But by the time he's dressed in his dad's tux, Rachel's date is there, and they're walking out the door. The tape ends on the face of a devastated Ross. But the present-day Ross has better luck: Rachel, touched by what she's seen, walks up to him and gives him a passionate kiss. All is forgiven.

February 8, 1996, "The One Where Ross and Rachel . . . You Know":

After a number of false starts, Ross and Rachel finally get intimate under the stars. Not the real stars, but the ones at the planetarium in the American Museum of Natural History. The next morning, after they've . . . you know . . . they awake to find themselves naked, inside a museum diorama, and being stared at by a group of curious schoolchildren. The deed is done. They are now an official couple.

A *TV Guide* Q&A with Jennifer Aniston and David Schwimmer

TV Guide: That episode where Ross and Rachel kissed for the first time [November 9] was very satisfying, from a fan's viewpoint. Was it a difficult scene for you two?

David Schwimmer: It was a huge moment. We took a lot of time working on the fight that came before it. It had to be hot. It had to be heated and it had to be irrational and it had to be romantic and it had to be sweet. All those things at the same time. But for me, it also had to be Ross being a man for the first time, just being *aggressive* in some way.

Jennifer Aniston: It was very intense to see the audience react the way they did, all the screaming and cheering. At one point David and I were hugging, and our hearts were just pounding, and we were both saying, "Can you *believe* this?" It was very wild. But we didn't actually nail that scene in front of the audience. It was almost as if we couldn't do it because all these people were watching. And when we shot it again after the show, it was able to really happen.

TV Guide: Were you as eager as everyone else to see them finally get together?

J.A.: Yeah, of course. I wanted to see what would happen. It'll take us down such a different road.

D.S.: My biggest concern is if you have all that sexual tension going on between two characters and then suddenly it's gone, then you really have to be prepared to address the "now what?" issue. You know, where do you go from here? I don't want the audience to be bored with Ross and Rachel now.

TV Guide: Would David ever be attracted to somebody like Rachel?

D.S.: I would be attracted to her, but I need someone who has direction, who's working toward something they're really passionate about. That's what turns me on and gets me going.

TV Guide: Would Jennifer ever be attracted to someone like Ross?

J.A.: Absolutely. Schwimmer looks a lot like my high-school sweetheart. So yeah, I'd be attracted to him. I love that sweet puppy-dog-eyed kind of thing.

This interview, by Susan Spillman, first appeared in a fall 1995 issue of TV Guide.

6

WHEN FRIENDS FIGHT

When Friends fight, things can get ugly. Pride can get wounded. Feelings can get hurt. Heads can get flicked. When Friends fight, there are repercussions. Secrets are revealed. Grudges are held. Muffins are licked. But when Friends fight, there is one thing you can always count on: a happy ending.

THE "GOT THE KEYS" FIGHT

Participants:

First Monica and Rachel, then everyone.

Theme:

Miscommunication. While Thanksgiving dinner is cooking, the gang runs out of the apartment to see a rogue Underdog balloon. When they return, they're locked out, and it's all . . . *somebody's* fault. Rachel blames Monica, because when they left Monica said, "Got the keys." Monica blames Rachel, because when they left she *asked*, "Got the keys?" As they stand there and argue, the turkey dinner is burned beyond recognition, and everyone blames everyone else for anything that ever went wrong.

Resolution:

Once they're back in the apartment (Joey had a spare set of keys), Phoebe spots Ugly Naked Guy having Thanksgiving dinner—with Ugly Naked Girl. The group is strangely moved ("There's gonna be some Ugly Naked Sex tonight," Chandler predicts), and, suddenly infused with the holiday spirit, spontaneous group forgiveness occurs.

THE BEASTLY FIGHT

Participants:

Ross and Marcel.

Theme:

Man's inhumanity to monkey? Ross thinks Marcel is mad at him for spending too much time at work. At the same time, Ross is angry because Marcel doesn't seem to be putting much effort into their relationship: "He's just phoning it in."

Them's Fightin' Words:

According to Ross, "I said some things I didn't mean. He threw some feces."

Resolution:

When Ross wakes up from a nap and finds the little guy snuggled up against him, he realizes that Marcel really does care.

THE MOTHER-KISSER FIGHT

Participants:

Ross, Joey, and Chandler.

Theme:

"Breaking the code," which is what Ross does when he kisses Chandler's mother (she kisses him back, by the way). When Joey catches the two, he's furious with Ross. When Ross confesses to Chandler, Chandler is furious with Ross. And when Chandler finds out that Joey knew but didn't tell him, he's furious with Joey.

Them's Fightin' Words:

Chandler calls Ross a "mother-kisser," grabs him by the finger, and pushes him out of Central Perk.

Resolution:

Joey forgives Ross because, well, Joey's not one to hold a grudge. And Chandler forgives Ross after his mother explains to him that she's always going to be wild and impetuous, and he might as well get used to it.

THE COMA GUY FIGHT

Participants:

Phoebe and Monica.

Theme:

Sneaking around behind your friend's back. Each girl suspects the other of doing just that in order to win the affections of Coma Guy, their unconscious dream man.

Resolution:

The fight comes to a sudden end when Coma Guy awakens—and turns out to be a total jerk.

THE MISTAKEN IDENTITY FIGHT

Participants:

Monica and Rachel.

Theme:

Deception and betrayal. When Rachel sprains her ankle, she asks Monica to switch identities with her at the hospital so she can use Monica's health insurance. Monica thinks it's a bad idea but agrees anyway. However, when the girls decide to go on a date with the doctors who treated Rachel, they must continue their charade, which leads to an outpouring of nasty "self"-revelations—and two very uncomfortable doctors.

Them's Fightin' Words:

Monica—as Rachel—tells the doctors that she's selfish, spoiled, and a former bed-wetter. Rachel—as Monica—reveals that she once shoplifted and was "a cow in high school."

Resolution:

Rachel admits that switching identities wasn't such a hot idea; apologies soon follow.

THE BAD BABY-SITTER FIGHT

Participants:

Ross and Rachel.

Theme:

Rachel's ineptitude, as demonstrated when she baby-sits Marcel: She leaves the apartment door open, and the monkey escapes.

Them's Fightin' Words:

A sarcastic Ross tells Rachel he blames himself for giving her such a difficult task: "I should have started you with, like, a pen or a pencil."

Resolution:

Ross forgives Rachel after she gets Marcel back by outsmarting the mean animal control woman.

THE EVOLUTION FIGHT

Participants:

Ross and Phoebe.

Theme:

Evolution: He believes in it, she doesn't—"Monkeys. Darwin. It's a nice story, but it just feels too easy."

Them's Fightin' Words:

Ross is dumbfounded that Phoebe doesn't accept evolution as a fact, like air or gravity. To which Phoebe replies, "Don't even get me *started* on gravity."

Resolution:

Phoebe wins the fight, not by disproving the theory of evolution but by getting Ross to admit that there's a "teeny-tiny chance" he's wrong. When he does, she proceeds to berate him for not standing his ground.

THE RICH GUYS, POOR GUYS FIGHT

Participants:

Ross, Monica, and Chandler versus Joey, Phoebe, and Rachel.

Theme:

Ross, Monica, and Chandler's lack of consideration for their economically challenged friends, as illustrated by the restaurant they choose to celebrate Monica's promotion. (Joey looks at the pricey menu and complains, "What are these, like, *famous* chickens?")

Them's Fightin' Words:

The argument comes to a head when the rich three try to treat the poor three to a Hootie & the Blowfish concert on Ross's birthday, which makes the poor three feel like they're part of a "Poor Friends Outreach Program." Phoebe speaks for all three when she declines, saying, "I'm just not in a very Hootie place right now."

Resolution:

The fight fizzles when Monica gets fired from her job and the rich-versus-poor balance is tipped.

THE SHOPPING SPREE FIGHT

Participants:

Monica and Rachel.

Theme:

Shopping with the enemy behind your friend's back, which is what Monica does when she goes on an outing with Ross's girlfriend Julie. When Rachel learns of this infidelity she is devastated, though a repentant Monica assures her that the outing meant nothing to her and that she was thinking of Rachel the whole time.

Them's Fightin' Words:

The fight gets ugly when Rachel asks the big question: "I have to know one thing: Did you go with her to Bloomingdale's?" Monica reluctantly nods her head, and Rachel storms off.

Resolution:

Rachel forgives Monica after a weepy Monica assures her that no one could ever steal her away from her: "You're my . . . we're . . . oh, I love you!"

The List Fight

Participants:

Ross and Rachel.

Theme:

Ross's insensitivity, as demonstrated by the list he makes of Rachel's and Julie's pros and cons.

Instigator:

Chandler, who tells Ross that a list will help him choose the right woman. (Joey, of course, doesn't think Ross needs to choose: "I got two words for you," he advises his friend. "Threesome.")

Feeble Attempts at Reconciliation:

Over the course of six episodes, Ross tries to make up to Rachel in the following ways: by reciting her pros (she cries at game shows, loves her friends, plays with her hair when she's nervous, is brave for starting over, is great with Ben, smells good); by dedicating a song to her on the radio; by giving her a Slinky; by letting her make a list about *him*; by calling her his lobster. All attempts are unsuccessful—even the Slinky one, believe it or not.

Resolution:

Rachel forgives Ross when she watches her old prom video and sees how hopelessly devoted he was to her, even then.

THE FLICKING FIGHT

Participants:

Monica and Rachel.

Theme:

Jean-Claude Van Damme. Rachel approaches him on behalf of a starstruck Monica but ends up setting up a date for herself.

Weapons of Choice:

Fingers. As Monica rants at Rachel for selling her out, Rachel flicks Monica on the forehead. The flick is returned, and so on, and so on, and so on.

Resolution:

Phoebe steps in and brings the girls to their knees with a Phoebe Death Grip. Rachel, under extreme duress, agrees to cancel her date with Van Damme and set Monica up with him instead. Phoebe, pleased with her handiwork, says, "If we were in prison, you'd be, like, my bitches."

THE HANDBAG MARINARA FIGHT

Participants:

Monica and Rachel.

Theme:

Jean-Claude Van Damme. True to her word, Rachel gets Van Damme to agree to a date with Monica—but she does so by telling him that Monica is dying to have a threesome with him and Drew Barrymore. Monica is not pleased.

Weapons of Choice:

A sweater and a purse. Back at the apartment, Monica demands an apology. Rachel refuses. Monica picks up Rachel's sweater, tugs on a loose thread, and threatens, "Say you're sorry or the sweater gets it." Rachel retaliates by grabbing Monica's purse and a jar of tomato sauce: "Give me the sweater, or it's handbag marinara." The fight escalates, and Monica unravels the sweater as Rachel pours the sauce.

Resolution:

Once again Phoebe intervenes, and the girls, repentant, apologize.

The Ugly Bracelet Fight

Participants:

Joey and Chandler.

Theme:

Dissing a friend behind his back, which is what Chandler does after Joey gives him an insanely ugly gold bracelet. Chandler sets the ball rolling when he goes to Central Perk and describes the bracelet to Phoebe as "the eyesore from the Liberace House of Crap." Joey stands behind him, listening to every word.

Feeble Attempts at Reconciliation:

Back at their apartment, Chandler apologizes to Joey, then suddenly notices he's no longer wearing the bracelet—it's lost. When Joey leaves the room,

Chandler searches the sofa, pulling off the cushions. Joey walks in on this scene, and Chandler, scrambling for an excuse, explains that he is holding the cushions as a symbol of his "sorrow and regret, just as they did in biblical times." Joey is unmoved.

Resolution:

As soon as Chandler buys a new bracelet to replace the lost one, the lost one turns up—and so does Joey. Chandler hands one over to him, saying it's a gift. Joey, touched, says the two of them are now "bracelet buddies." Chandler grins, bears it, and wears it.

THE BERT AND ERNIE FIGHT

Participants:

Joey and Chandler.

Theme:

Rejection and desertion. Chandler is crushed by the fact that Joey wants to get his own apartment.

Them's Fightin' Words:

Joey explains to Chandler that he doesn't *need* a roommate anymore. "It's not like we agreed to live together forever . . . we're not Bert and Ernie."

Resolution:

Things are chilly between the two until Joey's moving day arrives. Joey walks out of the apartment, leaving Chandler alone and despondent. Then he walks back in and gives Chandler a big hug. It's a very Bert and Ernie moment.

THE SIBLING FIGHT

Participants:

Ross and Monica.

Theme:

Stupid sibling stuff. Now that Ross is spending so much time over at Monica and Rachel's apartment, he's driving his sister nuts. He hogs the bathroom, he doesn't take phone messages, and he won't let Monica watch *Entertainment Tonight.* Ross thinks their spats are all in good fun, like when they were kids, but Monica reveals that she hated Ross when they were kids—he was mean, he teased her, and he always got his way. "And that wasn't fun for you?" Ross asks in disbelief.

Resolution:

Monica tells Ross that though she doesn't hate him anymore, he's got to stop bugging her. He agrees.

THE CONDOM FIGHT

Participants:

Monica and Rachel.

Theme:

Which girl deserves to get the last condom in the box.

Resolution:

At Rachel's suggestion, they flip for it: "Instruction side, I win. Little horse, you win." Rachel wins.

THE GODDESS FIGHT

Participants:

Monica, Rachel, and Phoebe.

Theme:

Cheating on a quiz, as in the "Goddess Quiz," found in the female empowerment book *Be Your Own Windkeeper.* As the girls accuse each other of answering the questions dishonestly, a fight escalates.

Them's Fightin' Words:

The girls, borrowing expressions from the book, hurl insults at each other. The name-calling starts with "leaf blower," "pool drainer," and "twig snapper" and ends with "monkey butt"—which *was* not in the book.

Resolution:

Rachel ends the fight by giving her girlfriends complimentary cake at the coffeehouse. Touched by the gesture, they all forgive one another and vow to not suck each other's wind anymore. (After which Rachel takes back the piece of cake.)

THE BANANA BRAN MUFFIN FIGHT

Participants:

Monica and Chandler.

Theme:

Selfishness, as exhibited by Chandler when Rachel brings over the last banana bran muffin. Monica ordered it first, but Chandler grabs it.

Weapon of Choice:

Tongues. When Monica demands that Chandler hand over the muffin, he does—but first he licks it. Monica refuses the licked muffin. In retaliation, she grabs the cup of coffee sitting in front of Chandler and licks the rim. She's enormously pleased with herself—until Chandler points out that the cup she licked was already on the table when he got there.

Resolution:

There is none. With luck Monica will forgive and forget.

7

UGLY NAKED GUY AND OTHER *FRIENDS* MYSTERIES

UGLY NAKED GUY: A REVEALING PORTRAIT

What do we *really* know about Ugly Naked Guy? Actually, quite a bit:

Handsome? No! Healthy? Yes!

On various occasions Ugly Naked Guy has been spotted using a Thighmaster, a Hula Hoop, and gravity boots.

He's a Sucker for Fads

See above.

He's Got Talent

He's got a penchant for making shadow puppets, and he does a remarkably lifelike Abraham Lincoln.

He's Handy Around the House

Ugly Naked Guy is a home-improvement buff (in

the buff, as it were), as witnessed by Monica in late 1994: "Oh, God help us," she cried, "Ugly Naked Guy is laying kitchen tile."

He's Resourceful . . .

Ugly Naked Guy keeps candles at the ready in case of emergency, as demonstrated in "The One with the Blackout."

. . . But He's Clumsy

Ugly Naked Guy burned himself lighting the aforementioned candles. On another occasion, he also managed to accidentally sit in some gravy.

He's a Chick Magnet

Ugly Naked Guy enjoyed Thanksgiving dinner with—who else?—Ugly Naked Girl. (They did, however, wear Pilgrim hats.)

He's Got a Funny Bone

In a wacky holiday mood, Ugly Naked Guy once hung candy canes in a "festive" place.

He's a Firm Believer in R&R

Ugly Naked Guy has taken at least one vacation. Curiously, he sported a tan line upon his return.

He's Got Culture

Ugly Naked Guy treats himself to cello lessons.

OTHER *FRIENDS* MYSTERIES: AN A TO (ALMOST) Z GUIDE

Ugly Naked Guy isn't the only guy in town. The *Friends* world is peopled with countless guys . . . not to mention girls and misters and misses and boys and men and ladies.

Amish Boy

Ross, who wants to use a pen and paper to make his list instead of Chandler's new laptop.

Aramis Guy

Joey, during his stint as a department store spritzer.

Arm Guy

What Chandler's boyhood friends called him during a particularly awkward growth spurt.

Asthma Guy

A model on a city free-clinic poster who Phoebe thinks is cute.

Balloon Guy

The man Monica buys balloons from to give to Coma Guy (see below).

Big Guy

What Ross calls Joey after he loses his role as Al Pacino's butt double.

Blond Girl

Phoebe, according to the Tattoo Artist.

Bobo the Sperm Guy

Ross, according to Susan, his ex-wife's lesbian lover.

Bug Lady

Ross's date, an insect curator at the American Museum of Natural History.

Butt Guy

What the director of the Al Pacino movie calls Joey.

Cheating Man

Ross, when he tries to use *garge* as a word during Scrabble (he claims it's a nautical term).

Chinese Menu Guy

Rachel's mom, when she knocks on the door at Rachel's birthday party (Monica only says she's the Menu Guy so Rachel's dad won't see her).

Coma Guy

The handsome stranger who gets hit by a car while being ogled by Monica and Phoebe.

Crazy Snake Man

Chandler's idea of how he'll end up—old and alone and with a snake, scaring all the neighborhood kids.

The Egg Lady

A neighbor of Ross's who once borrowed an egg; Chandler and Joey convince him to ask her on a date.

Famous Burma Tree Surgeon Guy

The way Phoebe thought of her real dad—until she found out that he was a pharmacist in upstate New York.

Flame Boy

A stage name that Phoebe suggests for Joey (after he gives up "Joseph Stalin").

The Frame Guy

Phoebe's fake father.

Gel Boy

Rachel's nasty nickname for Ross.

Guy with the Telescope

A neighbor of Monica and Rachel's.

Hombre Guy

Joey's duded-up rival at his department store job, who spritzes shoppers with Hombre cologne.

Horrible Woman

A woman who terrorizes Rachel over a laundry cart at the Launderama during her first "date" with Ross.

Joseph the Processing Guy

Joey's name for the "character" he plays when he's working at Chandler's office.

Library Guy

The cute guy who asks Phoebe to sing at the children's library.

Little Monkey Guy

Marcel.

Little Naked Guy

Ross, in a baby picture.

Mean Guys

Bullies who steal Chandler's hat.

Miss Cranky Pants

Chandler says he once dated one.

Mr. Back-from-the-Orient

Ross.

Mr. Big Arms

Chandler (see "Arm Guy," above).

Mr. Cranky Pants

Ben, Ross's son.

Mr. Johnny New Eggs

Eddie, Chandler's temporary roommate, who's handy with the breakfast skillet.

Mr. Look-at-Me-I'm-Evolving

A caveman in a diorama that Ross is assembling at the museum.

Mr. Major Capade Guy

Phoebe's former husband, Duncan, who skates in the Ice Capades.

Mr. Suity-Man

Chandler, when he gets all dressed up to see a career counselor.

Monkey Boy

Rachel's other name for Ross.

Noisy Boys

Phoebe's soon-to-be-boyfriend and his colleague, whose conversation distracts her while she's singing.

Noisy Girl #1 and Noisy Girl #2

Rachel and Monica, as they are referred to by the late Mr. Heckles's lawyer.

Not-So-Blond Girl

Rachel, according to the Tattoo Artist.

Obsession Girl

A coworker of Joey's at the department store.

Orthodontist Guy

Barry, Rachel's ex-fiancé.

Pharmacist Guy

The way Phoebe thinks of her real dad now that she knows the truth.

Pig Man

Paolo, according to Rachel after he hits on Phoebe.

Pizza Guy

The pizza delivery boy.

Princess Bubble Yum

What Rachel looks like in her maid-of-honor gown for Barry and Mindy's wedding.

Psycho Cab Lady

A woman who fights Rachel for a cab.

Puppet Guy

Phoebe's ex-boyfriend, whom she let "wash his feet in her Pool of Inner Power."

Scary Scientist Man

Ross, when he tries to convince Phoebe that evolution is a fact.

Science Guy

David (a.k.a Noisy Boy), the scientist who briefly dates Phoebe until he had to fly to Minsk.

Screaming Guy

A person who rode on the bus in China with Ross and Julie.

Standing Man

What Ross calls baby Ben when he pulls himself up.

Submarine Guy

Phoebe's Navy-officer boyfriend.

Trekkie Guy

A dud date of Monica's.

Weird Girl

Phoebe, according to a homeless woman she tries to help out.

Wine Guy

Paul, who tricks Monica into sleeping with him by telling her he hasn't been able to perform since his wife left him.

8

FRIENDS BY THE NUMBERS

1 Number of shoes Marcel the monkey destroyed.
1 Number of women Richard Burke slept with before sleeping with Monica.
2 Number of women Ross slept with before sleeping with Rachel.
3 Number of times Chandler broke up with Janice.
3 Number of ways Monica prepares the first *Friends* Thanksgiving potatoes (whipped, lumpy, and in the form of tots).
4 Number of claps that come after the opening line of the *Friends* theme song.
5 Number of men Rachel has slept with.
6 Number of times Ross came "this close" to telling Rachel he loved her.
12 Number of blocks Richard Burke let Joey drive his Jag.
15 Number of blocks Richard Burke let Chandler drive his Jag.
42 Page number on which Joey's *Soap Opera Digest* feature begins.

79	Most memorable page of Mrs. Bing's book *Mistress Bitch*, legendary among Chandler's childhood friends.
97	Number of steps from Joey and Chandler's apartment to Central Perk.
317	Number of times Monica's prom date saw *Star Wars*.
400	Number of dollars Chandler spent to replace the ugly bracelet that Joey gave him.
1,200	Number of dollars Joey paid for a Lucite parrot when he was living large off his *Days of Our Lives* paychecks.
40,000	Number of dollars Rachel's parents spent on her nonwedding.
A lot	Number of men Monica slept with.

9

FRIENDS' FOLKS

How did the Friends get to be so . . . so . . . so uniquely *Friends*-ian? Yeah, yeah, yeah, it's easy to give credit to the people who invented them—say, the writers and creators of the series—but what about those dedicated men and women who raised the Friends: their moms, their dads, Phoebe's flaky grandmother? As the second season drew to a close, we spoke with the actors who portray the Friends' folks and asked them how they *really* feel about their television offspring. They answered like true parents: with love, with affection, and with just the occasional ego-fracturing remark (dressed up as constructive criticism).

MARLO THOMAS
(RACHEL'S MOM, SANDRA GREEN)

TV Guide: Why are you the perfect mother for Rachel?

Marlo Thomas: We look alike. We have the same coloring. Also, our hairdos became stars. It's almost like we have these pets, and they're our hair. They're living things, these hairdos. So Rachel and I have a lot in common. I think Rachel is very much like *That Girl* [Thomas's character in the hit series of the same name from the sixties]. She's got a lousy job. A funny job. What I really mean is, she can't do it well. She never gets the coffee right, or she serves it to the wrong person. That's kind of the way *That Girl* was, never good at any of her jobs. I played waitresses a lot of times, and I wasn't a good one, either. Being a good waitress is an art—I didn't have it, and neither does Rachel. The first time I was on the show she brought some coffee to Chandler, who said, "Is mine the one with the cigarette in it or the one with lipstick on the cup?"

TV Guide: What do you think about the crowd she hangs out with?

M.T.: I'm happy she has friends like that. Because they're fun, and they're not jealous of each other; they're not competitive. They're so different that they each can offer different insights. I mean, who in the world thinks like Phoebe? Everyone needs a Phoebe to get that kind of angle in their lives. And Chandler has such a wonderful fiendish, boyish way about him. He's so playful. And Joey is so innocent and guileless. That's what I like about all of them—they're innocent and good. None of them is taking advantage of any of the others or being exploitative in any way. And I think that's what every mother wants for her daughter—to have friends who like her for who she is.

TV Guide: What makes Rachel stand out from the crowd?

M.T.: It's her incredible warmth. I think she's very much a den mother type. She's sexy and adorable and all that, but she also has a kindness and a caring to her. You get the feeling that if somebody was in trouble, not only would she care enough, but she's capable enough to take care of the situation. She's not a flake in any way. She's got a really good head on her shoulders.

TV Guide: What qualities does Rachel have that only a mother could love?

M.T.: Oh, dear. I don't know. I'd be guessing.

TV Guide: Which of the Friends would you adopt in real life?

M.T.: I guess Joey. He seems like he needs a lot of taking care of.

TV Guide: Are you happy with the way your TV child turned out?

M.T.: Oh, yeah. I think the most important thing in the world is to be a person who cares about other people. And to be responsible. And she's both things. Somebody you can count on.

TV Guide: What's the best advice you could give her?

M.T.: I guess I'd want to help her find her way in her career. To help her with her interests so she could find a job that would best suit her talents.

TV Guide: What's the perfect career for Rachel?

M.T.: Rachel is wonderfully warm and caring, so I think she should be a social worker. If not that, she's so beautiful she should be a model. [Spoken like a true mother!]

RON LEIBMAN
(RACHEL'S DAD, DR. LEONARD GREEN)

TV Guide: How did you end up as Rachel's dad?

Ron Leibman: My twenty-three-year-old stepdaughter forced me. It looked like I wasn't going to be able to do it. I hadn't seen the show, but I had heard about it—I'm not media-deaf. But I had this message on my answering machine from my stepdaughter, which went, 'Ohmigod. Ohmigod. Ohmigod. You have to do it. Ohmigod, those kids. Ohmigod. I want to meet them. Ohmigod.' So I said, "If I want to be a hero in my own home, I better do it."

TV Guide: How can we tell that you and Rachel are both Greens?

R.L.: I could very well look like her. And Marlo

and I could be married. We've known each other for years. When I did the show, she came over to me and said, "I don't know why in God's name I would ever have left you." It was pretty cute.

TV Guide: What do you think about the crowd Rachel hangs out with?

R. L.: My reaction to them, as my character, was not too friendly. He thought that they were very strange kids, because they were acting strangely that night. Of course they were: They were trying to hide him from his wife. They were pushing him all over the place.

TV Guide: What makes your kid stand out from the crowd?

R. L.: She's vivacious, smart, sweet, bright. Dr. Green would say she's a classy girl, much classier than those bums she's hanging around.

TV Guide: What qualities does Rachel have that only a father could love?

R. L.: She's very sensitive. She needs fathering. I don't know if Dr. Green is capable of it, but I am.

TV Guide: Which of the Friends would you adopt in real life?

R. L.: Rachel. Absolutely. Because she reminds me of my stepdaughter. She's really a darling girl.

TV Guide: Are you happy with the way your TV child turned out?

R. L.: Yeah, to a certain extent. I think he'd [Dr. Green] like for her to be doing more than waiting on tables. Like any pushy father. Of course, he's more concerned with his own feelings about his estranged wife. He seems to be pretty selfish. He's not *Father Knows Best.* He's acerbic, hard-edged. But he does have a very soft spot for his daughter.

TV Guide: How would you father her?

R. L.: Give her a hug. A lot of hugs. And sit and talk with her. Because when he [Dr. Green] talks with her, all he talks about are his pathetic problems. And he doesn't really ask her how she's doing. He's a very selfish character. He's rather colorful. He has more interest in his boat than he seems to have in his family. That's unfortunate for him, but it's a fun part to play. Who wants to play a boring character? He's rather flamboyant. Maybe that's why they chose me to play him.

MORGAN FAIRCHILD (CHANDLER'S MOM, NORA TYLER BING)

TV Guide: Why are you the perfect mother for Chandler?

Morgan Fairchild: I think there's a certain level of neuroses that Nora and Chandler both share. But I think she's a little more willing to go after what she wants, and he's still at the more insecure stage—which she threw out the window years ago. I think that part of it has made him fearful, and yet at the same time having a woman in his life as aggressive and free-spirited as Nora can also be a lot of fun—if he would ever let go and see it that way. I think he has a hard time doing it. I think when he caught my character kissing Ross it was a little tough.

TV Guide: What do you think about the crowd Chandler hangs out with?

M.F.: I think his friends are all lovely. In truth, any mother would be proud for her child to have such a nice support group in a big city like New York. I think Nora quite likes them and obviously was rather infatuated with Ross. I think she would love to see Chandler be more adventurous and take more chances, because that's the choice she's made in life. Although we always wonder if maybe she's had second thoughts about some of the things she's done with her life. But I think she understands his confusion more than he would think she does.

TV Guide: What makes Chandler stand out from the crowd?

M.F.: Well, he is the brightest, of course. He has a wonderful vulnerability and sensitivity, and I think that I would be very proud as a nineties mom to have brought up a young man who isn't a macho freak.

TV Guide: What qualities does he have that only a mother could love?

M.F.: He does get a bit obsessive, I think, especially in relation to his mother. I think she wishes he'd just let go of it every once in a while and just have fun. Nora would like for them to be pals, as opposed to Chandler always lecturing her on what she's done wrong.

TV Guide: Which of the Friends would you adopt in real life?

M.F.: Oh, Chandler. Definitely Chandler. I adore him.

TV Guide: So you're happy with the way he turned out?

M.F.: Definitely. I think he's got a great future in front of him—even though on the show they go through a lot of angst. He has good manners and a good sense of values, a good head on his shoulders and a great sense of humor. I think he's ready to tackle the world.

TV Guide: What's the best advice you could give Chandler?

M.F.: Get out of the building more often. Meet people. New York is a big town—you can go all over the place. You've got everything at your feet, you're young. There are so many things to do here that are fun when you're young and have the energy to do it.

And I'm not talking clubs—[I mean] the museums, the opera. That's the only thing I think that they're missing. They hang out at the coffeehouse all the time, which is fun, but let's drag him to *Carmen* one night! One night, come with Mom!

TV Guide: What kind of woman would be good for him?

M.F.: There's somebody out there for everybody. It just gets harder and harder to find them. The world has gotten so scattered. In Manhattan especially, he would need to find a girl who is not so caught up in the starry-eyed social whirl and would really appreciate him for what he has to offer, which is that vulnerability and caring and sensitivity. Someone who isn't just looking to be taken every night to fancy restaurants. Someone who truly cares about him. When you look at it, everybody on the show always seems to be trying to find somebody romantically and it never ever quite seems to work out. He's not alone in that boat. And the day they get married the show's over, so . . . no one's going to find happiness for very long.

TV Guide: Any plans to visit again soon?

M.F.: I'm kind of hoping I will, but I haven't heard from them. My "son" didn't write. Write your mother!

CHRISTINA PICKLES
(ROSS AND MONICA'S MOM, JUDY GELLER)

TV Guide: Who's your favorite, Ross or Monica?

Christina Pickles: Ross is a perfect son. He's a perfect boy. And Monica is taking a little longer. She has her problems, and my character has her problems with her. The bottom line is that they love each other and it will all work out. You know mothers and daughters. And of course their father is the sweetest man in the world, but thank God he has Judy. She keeps him focused. He's a dreamer.

TV Guide: Monica is worried that she's turning into her mother. Is she?

C.P.: We can only hope so.

TV Guide: What did Ross inherit from his mother?

C.P.: Ross sees things the way they are, the way she does. He's a very smart, sensible boy, and he copes well with the world, which hasn't always been easy on him. But look how well he does.

TV Guide: What do you think of the crowd they hang out with?

C.P.: I think they're the nicest kids I've ever been around. Ross seems to be happy with it, and whatever he's happy with, his mother is happy with. Monica seems to be growing from the experience of having good friends.

TV Guide: Is that new for her?

C.P.: She had her problems. I don't know if you saw the prom video—need I say more?

TV Guide: What makes your TV kids stand out from the crowd?

C.P.: They're my children! Ross is just perfect. And what a beauty Monica has turned into. The ugly duckling turned into a swan.

TV Guide: What qualities do Ross and Monica have that only a mother could love?

C.P.: What bad qualities? What do you mean, dear?

TV Guide: Which of the Friends would you adopt in real life?

C.P.: They're all irresistible! I can't play favorites. They're all so delicious, I'd have to take the whole bunch.

TV Guide: What's the best advice you could give Ross and Monica?

C.P.: Ross, keep on doing what you're doing, darling. Monica, maybe a career isn't the be-all and end-all. There's a lot to be said for a wonderful relationship like your father and mother have had all these years. A family.

TV Guide: How do you feel about Monica's current boyfriend, the Gellers' good friend Richard?

C.P.: Oh, please, what relationship? That's not a relationship! Richard's having a midlife crisis, and Monica's having temporary ridiculousness.

TV Guide: What kind of man would you like Monica to marry?

C.P.: Someone who's very good to her and loves her. And has lots of money.

TV Guide: Are you happy with the way your TV kids have turned out?

C.P.: Yes. How could I not be happy?

ELLIOTT GOULD (ROSS AND MONICA'S DAD, JACK GELLER)

TV Guide: What makes you the perfect dad for Ross and Monica?

Elliott Gould: All of the errors and mistakes that I made in judgment and perspective a generation ago make me a perfect father for them today.

TV Guide: What do you think about the crowd they hang out with?

E.G.: They're charming and interesting. Basically wholesome people.

TV Guide: What makes your TV kids stand out from the crowd?

E.G.: Do they stand out? No, I don't think they're any different from their friends—except that they are *our* children.

TV Guide: What qualities do Ross and Monica have that only a father could love?

E.G.: It's so interesting—Jack has to be careful not to be judgmental. He doesn't want to alienate them any further; he has to accept them for who they are and where they are, whether he likes it or not. Ross seems to be very talented and very indecisive. And very nice, very generous, very caring, very soulful. Very funny. A father's pride and joy. Monica seems to be different—far more unconventional as to what a typical parent would want for their daughter. She's not settling down; she seems to be living a life that is difficult for her parents to relate to. But she's a very good person, also very caring, very sensitive, and a very loving new woman.

TV Guide: Which of the Friends would you like to adopt?

E.G.: Well, already, it's almost as if our characters have adopted Rachel, since she's Monica's roommate. She's part of the family. And, whether we like it or not, everybody else is a part of the family, because that's the world in which these children are existing.

TV Guide: Who's your favorite, Ross or Monica?

E.G.: The writing from the beginning was that the parents seem to favor Ross and be harder on Monica.

TV Guide: How do you feel about Monica dating Richard?

E.G.: In the episode when Jack and Judy found out, the show was running long, so they cut out a delicious scene that was at the end. In it, I came to Monica's apartment and said I'd stopped by her boyfriend's place—I was going to give him a piece of my mind and punch him in the nose. But then he offered me a beer. It was so cool, he had a tap built into the wall. And again I was going to bring it up, but the football game was on. The gist of it is that I told her, "You're a big girl, you know what you're doing." He's a good guy, and even if it's an unconventional decision—and there's certainly a question as to what the future of their relationship is—it's in the moment, and I have no choice but to accept it.

TV Guide: Are you happy with the way Ross and Monica have turned out?

E.G.: I don't think they've turned out yet! My instinct is that I would trust Monica—that if I had a problem, Monica is the kind of caring daughter who would be there for her parents. And I'm sure that regardless of Ross's lack of self-esteem, he is always there for his parents. Therefore, this quality is maybe what they bring to their friends.

TV Guide: What's the best advice you could give your kids?

E.G.: Not to give up, and not to settle for anything less than peace and harmony.

ROBERT COSTANZO
(JOEY'S DAD, JOEY TRIBBIANI, SR.)

TV Guide: Why are you the perfect dad for Joey?

Robert Costanzo: I think the two Joeys are birds of a feather. They're both men who appreciate a well-turned ankle. And sometimes it gets them in trouble. But they're loyal. They love their families, but they're human.

TV Guide: What do you think of the crowd he hangs out with?

R.C.: What do I think of those kids? Well, they're all right. They're a lot different than the crowd Joey's dad grew up with—working-class guys just trying to survive and make a living. Some of the guys went bad, you know, they took the short cuts. Joey's dad has some bucks, his own business. He owns a chain of car washes or something like that. I do like the kids—I think they're great, got a lot of energy. They're diverse.

TV Guide: What makes Joey stand out from the crowd?

R.C.: He's a Tribbiani! Look at him. I think it's so

obvious that he's the Italian in the bunch. He's funny, he's brooding. He's got the vowel at the end of his name.

TV Guide: Should Joey Senior try to talk Joey Junior out of pursuing an acting career?

R.C.: Not at all—I think he's got the stuff. Not like half these guys out there trying to make it. He's sexy. He's funny. He's got what it takes. Although I do wish he'd consider going into the family business. But if not, I think he should forget about soap operas and go into feature films.

TV Guide: What qualities does Joey have that only a father could love?

R.C.: Joey's got a bit of a short temper. You apologize for him and then talk to him about it behind closed doors.

TV Guide: Which of the Friends would you adopt in real life?

R.C.: Besides Joey? Joey's such a great kid. If not him, maybe Chandler. You know, Joey sometimes gets out of hand at family occasions—he's not trying to please anybody. Whereas Chandler could be a game show host. Of the girls, I think Rachel.

TV Guide: Are you happy with the way your TV kid turned out?

R.C.: Yes, absolutely. He's a great kid.

TV Guide: What's the best advice you could give Joey?

R.C.: I wish he'd settle down. Who's available in that crowd right now? Phoebe? She's adorable. I'd love to see Joey get involved with her. She's great. She's very deep, and she seems a little more mystical than the other kids. She's a musician, right? I like her. I love her! I think they'd be great together. He should settle down. Except, well, there are always business trips. . . .

BRENDA VACCARO
(JOEY'S MOM, GLORIA TRIBBIANI)

TV Guide: Do you feel a familial bond to your TV son?

Brenda Vaccaro: Matt LeBlanc was adorable. He was the ultimate gentleman. He helped me. It was just like having this son—and when his "mom" did the show he wanted everything to be perfect. When he first saw me, his eyes got big; it was like I had just come down from Mt. Olympus. He was absolutely adorable. He told me I reminded him of his mother. What more can you ask for? Even though I never wanted to play a mother—I'd rather die than play a mother—I told myself, "You always think of yourself as a sex goddess." When you have to make the crossover, there's a part of you that goes, "Can I really do this? I have two Rottweilers and two cats! And a husband that's a lot younger than me. And I don't have children!" But what could be better than having all these young men adore me and treat me like a goddess? It's almost better than being young, my dear!

TV Guide: What do you think of the crowd Joey hangs out with?

B.V.: I think it's a really charming bunch of kids. They're charming and bright and talented.

TV Guide: What makes your TV kid stand out from that crowd?

B.V.: I think the way he dances. His hairdo is adorable. He was always quite a strutter, my boy. He's a neighborhood boy, and he never forgot where he came from. I also think he's got the cutest smile. He's got my smile. You seen my smile? Put a picture of our smiles together—he's got my smile. And he's got my good voice.

TV Guide: What do you think of Joey's acting career? Will he make it?

B.V.: I think he's gonna make it. But the struggle is long and hard, my dear. You know who he's gonna be? Marcello Mastroianni. He's the new Mastroianni. That's why his mom keeps pouring money into his career.

TV Guide: Which of the Friends would you adopt in real life?

B.V.: I would take them all as my little chicks, my little lambs, my babies. I would take them all! They're all a little piece of magic.

TV Guide: Are you happy with the way your TV child turned out?

B.V.: Fabulous! Fabulous! Couldn't be happier.

TV Guide: What's the best advice you could give Joey?

B.V.: Stay away from Brooke Shields! Stay away from the *Fatal Attraction* types.

AUDRA LINDLEY (PHOEBE'S GRANDMOTHER, FRANCES)

TV Guide: Why are you the perfect grandmother for Phoebe?

Audra Lindley: Well, we're both blondes. And people say she talks about her grandmother all the time, which pleases me very much.

TV Guide: How do you think your character's personality has affected Phoebe?

A.L.: I think Frances's liberalism has rubbed off. The fact that she's eccentric—a cab driver who dresses the way that she does—that certainly has rubbed off on Phoebe.

TV Guide: What do you think of the crowd she hangs out with?

A.L.: Those kids are absolutely wonderful. They're bright, terrific kids. Kids that age have gotten past the annoying stage and are developing into adults.

Frances has no objection to the crowd. She's a very liberal grandmother.

TV Guide: What makes Phoebe stand out from the crowd?

A.L.: She is honest, loving, totally without guile. She is so open and real. She's very sincere and a little bit more vulnerable than the rest of them. She's more easily victimized, too.

TV Guide: Do you think Phoebe's turbulent upbringing has made her more sensitive?

A.L.: I think losing her mother—her mother having been someone who practiced spiritualism—was very traumatic. That affects a child for the rest of her life.

TV Guide: What qualities does Phoebe have that only a grandmother could love?

A.L.: What is not to love about this girl? She is just terrific. She's perfect. Well, nobody's perfect, but I can't find the flaws.

TV Guide: Which of the Friends would you adopt in real life?

A.L.: Definitely Phoebe. I really felt that connection there as her grandmother. I would definitely adopt Phoebe. There was a strong pull, a strong affection.

TV Guide: Are you happy with the way Phoebe turned out?

A.L.: She's wonderful! I can't imagine having a more ideal granddaughter.

TV Guide: What's the best advice you could give Phoebe?

A.L.: Drive carefully.

10

THE COMPLETE *FRIENDS*

FIRST SEASON

The Pilot (first shown September 22, 1994)

A distressed Ross shows up at Central Perk with alarming news: His wife just dumped him for another woman. A distressed Rachel shows up soon after: She just dumped her fiancé at the altar. Meanwhile, Monica has a date with the seriously slimy Wine Guy.

"The One with the Sonogram at the End" (first shown September 29, 1994)

Ross learns that his lesbian ex-wife is pregnant with his child. Monica clings to the hope that Ross's news will give her mother something to do besides criticize her (dream on, Mon). Rachel has to return her engagement ring to ex-fiancé Barry—but first she has to find it. (Guest stars: Elliott Gould as Jack Geller; Christina Pickles as Judy Geller)

"The One with the Thumb" (first shown October 6, 1994)

Monica is afraid to let the other Friends meet her new boyfriend, Alan, but they love him—a bit *too* much, in fact. Phoebe is irritated because her bank keeps putting extra money in her account (oh, yes, and she also finds a thumb in a can of soda, "floating there like this tiny hitchhiker"). And Chandler takes up smoking again after three years on the wagon.

"The One with George Stephanopoulos" (first shown October 13, 1994)

Ross is depressed on the anniversary of the first time he ever had sex with his ex-wife Carol. Joey and Chandler try to cheer him up by taking him to a hockey game. It doesn't work. And Rachel is depressed by the small size of her first paycheck. Monica and Phoebe try to cheer her up with Twister and Tiki Death Punch but instead wind up depressed themselves—until they mistakenly receive what may be George Stephanopoulos's pizza.

"The One with the East German Laundry Detergent" (first shown October 20, 1994)

Breaking up is hard to do, so Phoebe and Chandler agree to terminate their respective relationships together. (Oh, Chandler, don't you know you can't get rid of Janice that easily?) Joey scams Monica into helping him rip another couple apart so he can pick up one of the pieces. Meanwhile, Ross and Rachel have their first "date"—at the Launderama.

"The One with the Butt" (first shown October 27, 1994)

After his stunning performance in *Freud!* (the musical), Joey lands a part as a part of Al Pacino—his butt—but overacts the role. Meanwhile, Chandler has an incredible relationship with a beautiful woman. There are just a few little problems: her husband and her other boyfriend.

"The One with the Blackout" (first shown November 3, 1994)

A power outage plunges New York into darkness—and traps Chandler in an ATM vestibule with a Victoria's Secret model. Ross attempts to tell Rachel his little secret, but a cat interferes. Then Paolo pops onto the scene, and when the lights come back on, he and Rachel are caught in a major lip lock. (Guest star: Jill Goodacre Connick)

"The One Where Nana Dies Twice" (first shown November 10, 1994)

Chandler's coworkers think he's gay, and the gang agrees that he has a certain . . . "quality." After Ross's and Monica's grandmother dies (twice!), Ross makes a grave mistake at the funeral, and Joey watches a football game.

"The One Where Underdog Gets Away" (first shown November 17, 1994)

Ross demands quality time with his unborn child. Joey's modeling gig as a poster boy gives him much more exposure than he likes. All of the Friends plan to get away on Thanksgiving, but the only one who does is Underdog—from the Macy's parade.

"The One with the Monkey" (first shown December 15, 1994)

As the holidays approach, the Friends make a solemn pact: no dates on New Year's Eve. But when Phoebe falls hard for Science Guy, the pact goes kaput—and Chandler must resort to desperate measures, setting up a date with Janice. And introducing the seventh Friend: Marcel. (Guest star: Hank Azaria as David)

"The One with Mrs. Bing" (first shown January 5, 1995)

Monica and Phoebe vie for the affections of their dream man, who doesn't know they're alive (he's in a coma). Chandler is mortified when his mother, the famous author, comes to town. Ross "breaks the code" by kissing his friend's mom. (Guest stars: Morgan Fairchild as Nora Tyler Bing; Jay Leno as himself)

"The One with the Dozen Lasagnas" (first shown January 12, 1995)

Monica makes a dozen lasagnas for her aunt. Unfortunately, they're meat, and her aunt wanted vegetarian. Are Chandler and Joey ready for commitment—i.e., sharing the cost of a new table? Ross tries to *not* find out the sex of his unborn child (it's a boy). Paolo visits Phoebe for a massage (and a lot more).

"The One with the Boobies" (first shown January 19, 1995)

The gang has just one little problem with Phoebe's new boyfriend, the shrink: They hate him. Joey discovers his father is having an affair with a pet mortician, and Chandler discovers Rachel unclothed, setting off a chain of terrible retribution. (Guest stars: Brenda Vaccaro as Gloria Tribbiani; Fisher Stevens as Roger)

"The One with the Candy Hearts" (first shown February 9, 1995)

Instead of having dates on Valentine's Day, the

girls decide to build a boyfriend bonfire, which burns out of control. Enter three cute firemen. Joey talks Chandler into a blind date with a woman who turns out to be none other than Janice—aaaarrggghh!—and Ross's first official date in nine years is disrupted by the appearance of his ex-wife and her lesbian lover.

"The One with the Stoned Guy" (first shown February 16, 1995)

Offered a promotion, Chandler quits instead and tries to decide what he wants to do when he grows up. Ross's new girlfriend wants him to talk dirty to her; Joey tries to teach him how. And Monica's dream job as a chef goes up in pungent-smelling smoke. (Guest star: Jon Lovitz as Steve, the Stoned Guy)

"The One with Two Parts, Part 1" (first shown February 23, 1995)

When worlds collide: It's Phoebe's twin, Ursula, the ditzy waitress on *Mad About You*. They're identical, but Joey can tell them apart—Ursula's the "hot" one. Meanwhile, Ross has to be the mommy in Lamaze class, and Chandler has to fire an attractive employee (but gives her a raise instead). (Guest stars: Helen Hunt as Jamie Buchman; Leila Kenzle as Fran.)

"The One with Two Parts, Part 2" (first shown February 23, 1995)

Injured but uninsured, Rachel convinces Monica to swap identities with her at the hospital—which gets complicated when a pair of cute doctors ask them out. Joey's dilemma: romance with Ursula or friendship with Phoebe? A crisis with Marcel shows Ross he's ready for daddyhood. (Guest stars: George Clooney as Dr. Mitchell; Noah Wyle as Dr. Rosen)

"The One with All the Poker" (first shown March 2, 1995)

After poker lessons from Aunt Iris, the girls won't stop playing until they beat the boys . . . and Marcel won't stop playing "The Lion Sleeps Tonight" until Ross loses his mind. Meanwhile, Rachel has a chance at her dream job—a buyer for Saks. (Guest star: Beverly Garland as Aunt Iris)

"The One Where the Monkey Gets Away" (first shown March 9, 1995)

Just as Ross is about to tell Rachel how he really feels, she loses Marcel! The gang launches a search, but Joey and Chandler find a couple of sexy neighbors instead, and Phoebe finds a tranquilizer dart with her name on it.

“The One with the Evil Orthodontist” (first shown April 6, 1995)

Rachel lands in the orthodontist’s chair with her ex-fiancé, Barry (even though he’s now engaged to her ex–maid of honor, Mindy). Chandler finally finds a girl he likes, but he doesn’t want to seem needy (even though he is). And someone with a telescope is scoping the gang. (Guest star: Jennifer Grey as Mindy)

“The One with Fake Monica” (first shown April 27, 1995)

Someone has stolen Monica’s credit card—along with the life Monica thinks she wants to lead. Marcel’s sexual monkeyshines lead Ross to make a painful decision—and so we bid farewell to the seventh Friend. Chandler helps Joey choose a stage name: “Joseph Stalin.” (Guest stars: Claudia Shear as Fake Monica; Harry Shearer as Dr. Baldharar)

“The One with the Ick Factor” (first shown May 4, 1995)

When Phoebe becomes his temporary secretary, Chandler learns that his coworkers ridicule him behind his back. Meanwhile, Rachel has sexy dreams about Joey and Chandler; Monica has a fling with a *much* younger man.

"The One with the Birth" (first shown May 11, 1995)

Ross becomes a daddy, Carol becomes a mommy, and Rachel comes on to a cute doctor. Monica and Joey experience parental pangs, but Carol's lesbian life partner is still in the closet—*locked* in, that is, with Ross and Phoebe. (Guest star: Jonathan Silverman as Dr. Franzblau)

"The One Where Rachel Finds Out" (first shown May 18, 1995)

Chandler inadvertently spills the beans to birthday girl Rachel about Ross's true feelings, but Ross has been suddenly called away to China ("It's a whole big bone thing"). Rachel dashes to the airport, but she's late for her appointment with fate. Meanwhile, Joey—who's giving his all for a fertility study—learns a new way to relate to a woman.

Second Season

"The One with Ross's New Girlfriend" (first shown September 21, 1995)

Now that she knows Ross loves her, Rachel goes to meet him as he returns from China. Too bad he's brought a new girlfriend, Julie, back with him. Meanwhile, Phoebe is persuaded to cut Monica's hair like Demi Moore's (whom Pheebs thinks is the guy in *Arthur*), and Joey learns that his tailor is a *very* naughty man. (Guest star: Lauren Tom as Julie)

"The One with the Breast Milk" (first shown September 28, 1995)

The guys are uncomfortable with Carol's breast milk—and Rachel is uncomfortable with Monica's growing friendship with Julie. Meanwhile, in the aisles of a great metropolitan department store, Joey tests his manhood in a showdown with a rival cologne-spritzing guy.

"The One Where Heckles Dies" (first shown October 5, 1995)

Dyspeptic downstairs neighbor Heckles dies, leaving the Friends his worldly goods—among which Rachel finds a lamp that Monica hates. Meanwhile, Chandler finds eerie parallels to his own life that convince him he is doomed to die a lonely loser. In desperation, he calls his dreaded ex, Janice. Phoebe and Ross have a bitter dispute over the theory of evolution.

"The One with Phoebe's Husband" (first shown October 12, 1995)

The gang is amazed to learn that Phoebe's *married*—to a gay ice dancer who's not so gay after all—and even more amazed to learn Chandler has a third nipple. Rachel gives Ross (supposedly) helpful advice on having sex with Julie.

"The One with Five Steaks and an Eggplant" (first shown October 19, 1995)

When a sexy woman calls the wrong number, Chandler seeks to make the most of the situation. Income disparity separates the Friends into two camps: the flush Ross, Monica, and Chandler versus the not-so-flush Phoebe, Joey, and Rachel. Monica gets a hickey from a Blowfish and loses her job (but that has nothing to do with the hickey).

"The One with the Baby on the Bus" (first shown November 2, 1995)

Oops: Chandler and Joey lose baby Ben while scoping babes on a bus, and Phoebe loses her gig at Central Perk to a *professional* singer. Ross has an allergic reaction to Monica's kiwi-lime pie, revealing his terror of hypodermic needles. And for the finale: a duet rendition of "Smelly Cat." (Guest stars: Chrissie Hynde as the new singer; Lea Thompson as Caroline)

"The One Where Ross Finds Out" (first shown November 9, 1995)

Monica takes on a new job—Chandler's own

personal fitness trainer—and Chandler is *so* not happy about it. Phoebe has a hard time trying to get her new boyfriend to have sex with her, but she finally succeeds. And, most important, Ross finds out that Rachel loves him—via a drunken phone message she left on his machine during a date with another guy. At the episode's end, they finally come together for a colossal kiss at Central Perk.

"The One with the List" (first shown November 16, 1995)

Ross has to choose between Rachel and Julie, and—with the help of Chandler and his new computer—lists the pros and cons of each. *Big* mistake. Meanwhile, Monica gets a new job: making Thanksgiving recipes for a synthetic (and inedible) chocolate substitute called Mockolate. Mockolate chip cookies, anyone? (Guest star: Michael McKean as Mr. Rastatter)

"The One with Phoebe's Dad" (first shown December 14, 1995)

It's Christmas time, and a broke Monica tries tipping with cookies instead of cash, with mixed results. Phoebe learns that the guy in all the picture frames her grandmother keeps around is not her dad after all and tries to track down her real father. Joey and Chandler put off their holiday shopping way too long, and after Ross breaks the knob on the radiator, there's a Christmas party with a tropical theme. (Guest star: Audra Lindley as Phoebe's grandmother)

"The One with Russ" (first shown January 4, 1996)

Monica gets back together with Fun Bobby, but when he stops drinking, she discovers he's not so . . . fun. Joey wins the role of Dr. Drake Ramoray, neurosurgeon, on *Days of Our Lives.* Rachel, dating a guy named Russ, is the only one who can't see his uncanny resemblance to Ross. (Guest star: "Snaro," aka David Schwimmer, as Russ)

"The One with the Lesbian Wedding" (first shown January 18, 1996)

Ross's ex and her lesbian life partner tie the knot, providing Monica with a job: catering the wedding. Phoebe is possessed by the spirit of an eighty-two-year-old massage client who dies in the middle of a session. Mrs. Adelman cannot rest until she's "seen everything" (needless to say, her spirit departs after attending the lesbian wedding). Rachel's mom comes to visit and drops a bomb: She's breaking up with Rachel's dad. (Guest stars: Marlo Thomas as Sandra Green; Candice Gingrich as the minister)

"The One after the Super Bowl, Parts 1 and 2" (first shown January 28, 1996)

It's a deluxe, star-studded, hour-long *Friends*! The search for Marcel leads the gang to the set of Jean-Claude Van Damme's new movie, where Rachel and Monica vie for the attention of the Muscles from Brussels. Joey dates a soap fan who has trouble distinguishing *Days of Our Lives* from real life. Phoebe sings for an audience of delighted children and appalled parents, and falls for a handsome musician. Chandler meets an old schoolmate: a makeup artist who *seems* hot for him despite the fact that he pulled her skirt up back in the fourth grade. (Guest stars: Brooke Shields as Erika Ford; Julia Roberts as Susie Moss; Jean-Claude Van Damme as himself; Chris Isaak as Rob Donnen)

•

"The One with the Prom Video" (first shown February 1, 1996)

As a token of his esteem, Joey gives Chandler a seriously tacky bracelet; meanwhile, an unemployed Monica is hard up for money. Then a blast from the past: a vintage video reveals Monica's former girth, Rachel's former nose, and the way Ross has always felt about Rachel. After seeing this touching scenario, Rachel gives Ross a passionate kiss.

"The One Where Ross and Rachel . . . You Know" (first shown February 8, 1996)

When Joey buys two reclining chairs and a super-jumbo TV, he and Chandler adapt a new lifestyle: complete immobility. Catering a party for her parents' friend Richard, Monica becomes what Phoebe calls "a smitten kitten." And amid the romantic ambiance of a planetarium, Ross and Rachel *finally* . . . you know. (Guest star: Tom Selleck as Richard)

"The One Where Joey Moves Out" (first shown February 15, 1996)

It's breakup time for *Friends'* most devoted couple—Joey and Chandler—and tattoos for two: Rachel and Phoebe. For his birthday, Monica's dad receives a special gift in the bathroom (with Monica as an unwilling witness) and the unsettling news that Richard's young "twinkie" is . . . Monica.

"The One Where Eddie Moves In" (first shown February 22, 1996)

After Phoebe is discovered by a record producer, it's "Smelly Cat" the video! Ross's new relationship with Rachel makes Monica feel like she's living with her brother all over again, and she hates it. Joey considers moving back in with Chandler, but Chandler has a *new* roommate! (Guest star: Adam Goldberg as Eddie)

"The One Where Dr. Ramoray Dies" (first shown March 21, 1996)

Joey finds out the hard way that it's not good to boast that you write your own soap dialogue: His character gets dropped down an elevator shaft. Phoebe helps Chandler bond with his new roommate . . . much to Chandler's horror. Sexual history dominates the discussion between two couples—Monica and Richard, and Rachel and Ross—and prompts a conflict over a condom.

"The One Where Eddie Won't Go" (first shown March 28, 1996)

Creeped out by his bizarre new roommate, Eddie, Chandler demands he move out. Eddie agrees . . . but doesn't leave. A new book on empowerment for women inspires the female Friends to have a "Goddess meeting." Joey has trouble coming to grips with the death of Dr. Drake Ramoray and the accompanying change in his lifestyle.

"The One Where Old Yeller Dies" (first shown April 4, 1996)

Phoebe's world view is shattered when she learns how *Old Yeller really* ends. Monica becomes jealous when Richard starts going out with other people—i.e., Joey and Chandler; and Rachel is upset to learn that Ross has planned their whole life together.

"The One with the Bullies" (first shown April 25, 1996)

Two bullies seize Ross and Chandler's turf—and Chandler's hat—at Central Perk, while Monica sets out to conquer Wall Street with her last $127. "Dad-hunting" once again, Phoebe instead meets a surprise sibling and a small but very nasty dog. (Guest stars: Peter DeLuise as a bully; Laraine Newman as Mrs. Buffay)

"The One with the Two Parties" (first shown May 2, 1996)

The gang plans a surprise party for Rachel's birthday, but the *real* surprise is when both her estranged parents show up. "Think!" urges Chandler. "What would Jack and Chrissy do?" Why, split it into *two* parties, of course—one for each parent. But complications inevitably ensue. . . .

"The One with the Chicken Pox" (first shown May 9, 1996)

An itchy situation: Just as her hunky Navy Guy surfaces for the first time in two years, Phoebe catches chicken pox from baby Ben! Joey pretends to be a data processor but gets a little too far into character. Richard needs to find an obsession in order to keep up with all of Monica's. (Guest star: Charlie Sheen as Ryan)

"The One with Barry and Mindy's Wedding" (first shown May 16, 1996)

Rachel agrees to be maid of honor at her ex-fiancé's wedding, but a fashion faux pas focuses attention away from the bride. To get a part, Joey needs practice kissing . . . guys. Monica ponders her future with Richard, and Chandler falls for a mystery woman on the Internet—who turns out to be Janice! (Guest star: Maggie Wheeler as Janice)

Amy Paulsen is deputy editor of *TV Guide* and a regular correspondent for *The Gossip Show* on E! Entertainment Television. She lives in New York City with her husband, Albert Nalle, and their two daughters, Nora and Rose.